US Foreign Policy in the Age of Trump

This book investigates the drivers, tactics, and strategy that propel the Trump administration's foreign policy.

The key objective of this book is to look beyond the 'noise' of the Trump presidency in order to elucidate and make sense of contemporary US foreign policy. It examines the long-standing convictions of the president and the brutal worldview that he applies to US foreign policy; and his hard-line negotiation tactics and employment of unpredictability to keep America's major foreign interlocutors off-guard, such as NATO members, China, Mexico, Canada, North Korea, and Iran – each of which are considered here. In strategy terms, the book explains that the president is responding to a new multipolar structure of power by engaging a Kissingerian strategy that eschews liberal values and seeks to adjust great power relations in Washington's favor. By drawing upon a range of evidence and case studies, this book makes a number of compelling and provocative points to offer a new vector for debate about the workings, successes and failures, and ultimately the long-term implications for the world, of the Trump presidency.

This book will be of much interest to students of US foreign policy, security studies, and IR in general.

Reuben Steff is Senior Lecturer at the University of Waikato, New Zealand.

US Foreign Policy in the Age of Trump

Drivers, Strategy and Tactics

Reuben Steff

 Routledge
Taylor & Francis Group

LONDON AND NEW YORK

First published 2021
by Routledge
2 Park Square, Milton Park, Abingdon, Oxon OX14 4RN

and by Routledge
52 Vanderbilt Avenue, New York, NY 10017

Routledge is an imprint of the Taylor & Francis Group, an informa business

British Library Cataloguing-in-Publication Data
A catalogue record for this book is available from the British
Library

Library of Congress Cataloging-in-Publication Data
Names: Steff, Reuben, author.
Title: US foreign policy in the age of Trump : drivers, strategy
and tactics/Reuben Steff.
Description: New York : Routledge, 2021. | Includes
bibliographical references and index.
Identifiers: LCCN 2020018228 (print) | LCCN 2020018229
(ebook) | ISBN 9780367860936 (hardback) | ISBN
9781003016861 (ebook)
Subjects: LCSH: United States--Foreign relations--2017- |
National security--United States. | Trump, Donald, 1946- |
World politics--21st century.
Classification: LCC JZ1480 .S78 2021 (print) | LCC JZ1480
(ebook) | DDC 327.73--dc23
LC record available at https://lccn.loc.gov/2020018228
LC ebook record available at https://lccn.loc.gov/2020018229

ISBN: 978-0-367-86093-6 (hbk)
ISBN: 978-0-367-55721-8 (pbk)
ISBN: 978-1-003-01686-1 (ebk)

Typeset in Times New Roman
by MPS Limited, Dehradun

Contents

1 'America first' as permanent destabilization
Deciphering the Trump administration's foreign policy

Introduction

Donald Trump's presidency is unlike that of any previous US administration. Without exaggeration the Trump administration is both disruptive and iconoclastic. And given the tendency of the president to lie, dissimulate, distract, offend, and contradict himself through a torrent of verbiage, discerning the reasons for such unprecedented behavior is stretching the analytical capacity of scholars. This may very well be intentional, as this book will reveal. It shows that the president is committed to projecting an image of himself as an unpredictable actor, and senior administration officials assert that working to destabilize world affairs is now in the US national interest (Goldberg, 2018). In essence, together they appear to believe that injecting an element of unpredictability and a feeling of permanent destabilization into international affairs will redound in America's favor, giving it leverage across a range of issues. As such, amidst the cacophony of the Trump presidency, is it possible to unearth the logic behind his foreign policy? Are the tactics and strategy a product of the president's supposedly unique business acumen, driven by ideological conviction, the unique qualities of Trump the individual and the domestic political imperatives he faces, or are they due to international systemic challenges? Alternatively, perhaps it is a combination of all of these.

A review of the existing literature that interrogates the Trump administration's foreign policy drivers can be broken down into two basic frames. These are domestic factors (including the president's personal worldview) and the international system/balance of power. Scholars that emphasize the latter have usually tended to connect their analysis to domestic considerations as well, suggesting a collapsing gap between the domestic and international levels. With that in mind, this book makes a novel contribution to the existing literature on contemporary US foreign policy in two ways. The first results from a synthesized and multi-level consideration of the drivers and underlying logic of the Trump administration's foreign policy tactics and strategy. Here, it draws upon the three levels of analysis (also known as frames) approach to international relations and international security issues proposed by Kenneth Waltz (Waltz, 1954). These include the *individual level* that focuses on the president, his personality and behavior; the *domestic level*, which emphasizes the need to consider the role of domestic drivers and factors in influencing foreign policy; and the *international level*, whereby structural forces generate incentives that influence US presidents. The book, through synthesis across these levels, makes a case that the Trump administration's tactics and strategy are a product of President Trump's personal stamp *and* the structural forces at the national and international levels which he, as with all US presidents, is responding to in foreign policy.[1] It also highlights the difficulty in clearly discerning whether the domestic level or international structure has greater sway in terms of influencing Trump's foreign policy.

The second novel contribution is through an articulation of the methods utilized by the president and an evaluation of whether they have been able to achieve his stated goals in the global arena, enhancing our understanding of the policy outcomes US diplomacy is attempting to achieve. In an environment that often takes its analysis on every individual foreign policy decision in isolation, it can be beneficial to survey the policy record of the administration across the fuller thematic and temporal scope of the government. Taking a broader view of the decisions the Trump administration has made in pursuit of its agenda clarifies the patterns and priorities which are evident in the decision-making structure of the administration's foreign policy apparatus. It also provides an insight into whether the president will continue to use his preferred methods and whether they could proliferate throughout the international system, with perceived successes breeding mimicry. The implications of this for interstate behavior would be immense.

Before proceeding, a caveat is in order. It is clear that any analysis of President Trump – given his peculiarities and penchant to lie and deceive (perhaps even to practice self-deception) – is likely to find itself challenged by the style and method through which Trump conducts his affairs. The scholar has to ask how much agency they should attribute to the president, how much of what he does and says is the result of a deliberate, calculating agenda, and how much is the product of an impulsive and chaotic mind. Yet, the historical record shows the president has a number of long-standing convictions and ideas about important international issues, and he is fiercely determined to pursue whatever end he sets himself. Having employed certain methods to (generally) be successful as a businessman prior to his presidency, and seemingly convinced of his own genius and the power of his agency to change global arrangements in his preferred direction, it was always likely that the patterns of behavior from his pre-presidential tenure would carry through into his time in office. As such this book takes Trump seriously, even if not literally all the time and in a point of departure from many analyses on the Trump presidency it imputes a greater level of tactical and strategic decision making on behalf of the president, even as it admits we may never truly know his mentation to the degree we think we understand those of other presidents. This account does not express support for the president's policies or operating style. Rather, it seeks to outline and consider his personal characteristics in a more objective manner than is typical in contemporary scholarship, and the interrelationship between the president and domestic and international forces. In doing so the arguments and evidence presented throughout offer an interesting, new vector for debate in the international relations literature about the workings, successes and failures, and ultimately the long-term implications for the world, of the Trump presidency.

Interrogating US foreign policy: Widespread criticisms and realist hopes

Critique of Trump's foreign policy has been widespread in international relations scholarship and extends across the American foreign policy establishment.[2] Many from this group adhere to liberal international relations precepts that, collectively, they believe should be the fundamental lodestar that guides Washington's international conduct (Sanger and Haberman, 2016; Brands, 2017a, 2017b, 2018; Mazarr, 2017; Walt, 2017; Daalder and Lindsay, 2018; Goldgeier, 2018; Ikenberry, 2018; Lissner and Rapp-Hooper, 2018; Norrlof, 2018; Stokes, 2018; Sullivan, 2018; Powaski, 2019; Herbert, McCrisken, and Wroe, 2019; Glasser, Preble, and Thrall, 2019). They hold that US efforts to create a liberal international order in the wake of World War II served American interests well, enabling it to fend off a challenge from Communism throughout the Cold War and cementing US power and influence. This project involved forging an open global economy facilitating win–win interactions, establishing multilateral institutions that increased cooperation and (to a degree) leveled the playing field between large and small states, advancing America's domestic values by promoting democracy, human rights and expanding the sphere of liberal democracies. Finally, US diplomacy established ostensibly permanent security alliances that carried American influence and power into a number of key regions. In effect, through this process, the US national interest became synonymous with the global interest.

The reasons so many scholars and officials oppose and criticize Trump's foreign policy should then be obvious. After all, as this book recounts, the president has questioned virtually every aspect of the liberal international project. He also has clear autocratic tendencies through which he views himself as the decisive agent of policy change in the US system. This overlays a zero-sum dog-eat-dog view of the social world that leads him to diligently seek to shift the balance of various international arrangements and settings in Washington's favor, even if it comes at the expense of America's allies and partners. Additionally, many in the American foreign policy establishment and at the highest political levels consider the US to be an exceptional nation not just because of its immense material capabilities but due to its mission to uphold and spread democracy worldwide; it is the key moral force for righteousness and justice in the world. These ideas are at stark odds with President Trump's preference for a cut-throat, ideologically ambivalent, transactional-style foreign policy. Trump has also proposed that the only thing that makes America exceptional is its material power, and that enhancing this should be the primary focus of US foreign policy (Edwards, 2018). Other elements of US influence, for example its soft power and liberal ideology, are ineffectual and should be cast into the dustbin of history. In Trump's world, amassing American might will ensure it remains pre-eminent.

Hal Brands argues that the starkest vision of Trump foreign policy – which would constitute 'Fortress America' – "would shred the international order that Washington has long promoted" (Brands, 2017a, 81). Additionally, Trump's strategy could drive some US allies and partners away from Washington (Brands, 2017b, 31). As such, gains from Trump's foreign policy would only be short term in nature, coming at the expense of America's long-term security. Another evaluation is that Trump's foreign policy is generally devoid of strategy (Kaine, 2017; Huxley and Schreer, 2017; Larres, 2017; Brands, 2017a; Lissner and Rapp-Hooper, 2018). Instead, there is evidence of a "tactical-transactional approach" (Lissner and Rapp-Hooper, 2018, 8). This overlaps with Trump's penchant to act unpredictably. Unlike Obama, for example, who projected an image of trustworthiness and certainty, Trump believes flexibility and erratic behavior to be virtues that keep others off-guard, as well as allowing the US to rapidly shift direction and seize the initiative when necessary.

Other scholars, primarily from the 'realist' school of international relations, take a different tack (Hoover, 2016; Mearsheimer, 2016; Rovere, 2016; Dueck, 2017, 2019; Friedman, 2017; Herman, 2017; Layne, 2017; Friedman, 2018; Schweller, 2018a, 2018b, 2018c; Anton, 2019; Blackwill, 2019). They charge that since the Cold War, US foreign policy has become unmoored from reality. To realists, the US must carefully discipline the use of American power to defend Washington's core interests such as the American homeland, reduce America's global military footprint to save costs, and shift to a position of 'offshore balancing' to guard against the emergence of great powers in Eurasia. In turn, it must compel US allies to do more. Instead of this, the US has acted like a revolutionary nation by pursuing a strategy of liberal hegemony – a strategy afforded it due to its position of primacy in a unipolar system where it was unchallenged by other great powers. According to many realists, Washington's leaders have too often been willing to intervene around the world in defense of, or to advance, liberal values. This has led the US to try to sustain a position of global primacy embedded through a worldwide forward-deployed military that ensures the US pays a disproportionately and unsustainably high cost for defense of the free world. In turn, this incentivizes allies and partners to do little other than make token contributions to the defense of the liberal rules-based international security order. Moreover, the well-intentioned objective of enlarging the sphere of liberal democracies through regime change has collided with reality, often leading to counter-reactions and reassertions of illiberal forces. The instability and war that followed in the wake of interventions and attempted 'nation-building' efforts in places like Afghanistan and Iraq (and Libya, albeit here US and allied efforts emphasized regime change through the use of air power and support to local rebel forces rather than deploy Western ground forces; 'nation-building' was not a priority) are evidence of this failed strategy, while the US has found itself bogged down in conflicts that have sapped its power and diverted its attention away from the political endgame – the need to manage relations among the great powers as a new international structure of multipolarity emerges. This is marked by the rise of China as a peer competitor to US power; a challenge which liberal hegemony, realists assert, is ill-suited to counter. As such, US grand strategy and foreign policy must quickly adjust, an opportunity afforded by President Trump's commitment to questioning the ideas that underpin liberal hegemony.[3] Therefore, while some of the realist persuasion are not convinced Trump is the kind of realist-in-chief they have been waiting for,[4] many of the president's foreign policy preferences align more closely with their assumptions and prescriptions. Furthermore, Trump's defense of what he calls 'principled realism' suggests he adheres to basic realist tenets (White House, 2017).

Situating this book in reference to the above literature, the book adheres to the view that international structure, which in a globalized system is linked to settings at the domestic level, generates powerful forces and incentives irrespective of whichever individual occupies the White House. Multipolarity must be reckoned with; at the same time, we need to recognize that the personality of President Trump is leaving a significant imprint on the methods and tactics the administration is using to pursue US interests. By using Waltz's three levels of analysis, the book advances the debate over the interrelationship of individual, domestic, and international factors on US foreign policy during the Trump presidency, and considers whether the administration's tactics and strategy are delivering success.

Chapter outline

The next chapter (Chapter 2) engages the *individual* and *domestic* levels of analysis. In doing so it firstly uses the individual level, outlining the preferences, behavior, and personality of the president to provide insight and understanding of US foreign policy. This draws attention to his worldview alongside the long-standing beliefs and convictions he holds on a number of issues germane to America's domestic affairs. These, in turn, relate to settings across the international system. Examining Trump's personality and psychology is insightful, revealing an individual who uses virtually any means available to achieve his ends given his brutal view of the world in which morals have little place. As such, rather than cloak the pursuit of the US's material interests behind ideology, Trump seeks to shed the US of its belief in American exceptionalism. The second frame allows a consideration of the domestic drivers and factors that influence the Trump administration's foreign policy. The chapter also makes the case, through a consideration of Trump's 2016 electoral strategy and tactics, that the president's behavior is rational, or at least rational enough, to achieve his ends albeit through a series of primarily tactical decisions. Having succeeded in virtually everything he put his mind to (despite the setbacks he experienced along the way), Trump undoubtedly saw his election as validation of his behavior and skillset, which he now applies to international relations.

Chapter 3 focuses on two key tactics, and extends the *individual* level of analysis. Firstly, it frames the chapter by explaining that Trump operates as a *tactical opportunist* before moving on to outline his negotiation methods and philosophy (the 'art of the deal'). It is clear the president consistently uses a certain style and method in his negotiations, and is waging a pressure campaign that involves amassing and applying US leverage against a number of US allies, partners, and adversaries.[5] The chapter draws upon insights from negotiation theory to outline and interrogate various features of this. Four cases in which his negotiation method is on display are then considered, involving the North Atlantic Treaty Organization (NATO), trade with China, Mexico and Canada, and negotiations over the North Korean nuclear program. Exploration of the second tactic, the president's commitment to unpredictability, is connected to ideas in the strategic studies literature (the 'rationality of irrationality'). In considering the results of these two tactics, the chapter finds they have produced some moderate short-term success, although they increase the risk of serious long-term costs – a topic discussed in Chapter 5. Furthermore, a pressure campaign, designed to extract concessions and improve America's national strength, is not inconsistent with the stresses that stem from the changing international structure: We could expect a superpower, fearing the continued loss of its influence, to employ methods in order to reduce the speed of its decline and attempt to position itself for a new period of dominance.

Chapter 4 draws upon the *international* level of analysis to show how the change in the structure of power towards multipolarity provides insight into US strategy, which increasingly displays elements of realpolitik or a Kissingerian strategy (indeed, the chapter makes the case Henry Kissinger may have played a role in this, further showing how structural and individual factors interact to produce outcomes). As unipolarity comes to an end, aspects of the president's behavior, such as his willingness to verbally praise authoritarian leaders, make sense beyond just a reflection of his own autocratic nature; they are explicable if seen as intent to provide the US with a greater level of foreign policy flexibility in an era of multipolarity. Downplaying America's role as a moral beacon and calling into question unending commitments to traditional alliances are consistent with this. Importantly, demonstrating that the US is not an ideological threat to autocratic states increases the prospect of these countries leaning towards the US at the expense of China and, in this context, the chapter considers the triangle of US–Russia–China relations. Preventing Russia from establishing a military alliance with China could prove critical to the future balance of power between Washington and Beijing. Opposition to Trump throughout the foreign policy establishment, the chapter explains, has prevented these efforts so far, providing a case study of how domestic actors can impede Washington's response to structural forces. Finally, the chapter considers whether US relations with authoritarian states and NATO allies have changed as a result of a narrowing understanding of the US national interest.

The fifth and concluding chapter reconsiders the agency versus structure debate in light of the analysis conducted throughout the book, suggesting areas where additional research could prove fruitful, and weighs up the outcomes from the president and his administration's efforts to alter international arrangements in Washington's favor. It then considers the implications of the president's tactics and contemporary US strategy for the future of the international system. Here, it suggests the president, through his global megaphone, is modeling hard-line negotiating behavior and unpredictability. Should other states perceive it to be successful, their leaders may emulate it, resulting in an increasingly unstable world. It also ponders whether the liberal international order will survive. Lastly, it offers some final reflections on the Trump presidency, explaining that the world, and America's place in it, stands at a pivotal inflection point and it remains an open question whether the president, gambling on an unorthodox approach to maximize American power, will prove successful in the long run.

Notes

1 For a discussion on the interrelationship between individual presidents and structural forces see Jervis (2013).
2 In March 2016 an open letter signed by 120 GOP-aligned national security experts was released that opposed Trump's presidency and his foreign policy on the grounds that it "make[s] America less safe, and which would diminish our standing in the world" (War on the Rocks, 2016). Additionally, 60% of the US State Department's top-ranking career diplomats have left since the Trump presidency began (Ordonez, 2018).
3 Polarity refers to the distribution of power between states throughout the international system. A system dominated by one state or center of power is a *unipolar* order, split between two is a *bipolar* order, and if three or more exist it is a *multipolar* order. The emergent system of multipolarity is one where no single state is in a position of dominance over all the other powers. The rise in power of China, especially, marks the emergence of multipolarity as Beijing becomes a near-peer competitor to the United States. See Wohlforth (2011) and Brooks and Wohlforth (2015/2016).
4 Stephen Walt (2016, 2017), a prominent realist, has strongly criticized Trump; Robert Jervis (2018, 5) has stated "a Trump foreign policy that follows his campaign statements would be hard to square with realism, although it would be difficult to say which alternative theory, if any, it

vindicated"; and Brian Rathbun (2018, 100) has also questioned Trump, stating that an "awareness of others' interests is at the heart of realpolitik" and Trump's disregard for others' interests "drives realists most crazy". Chapter 2 of this book notes that Trump does appreciate others' interests, but he only cares about them to the degree he can use the knowledge to exploit the other actors to pursue his own interests.

5 Colin Dueck characterizes the "Trump doctrine as a set of international pressure campaigns" (Dueck, 2019, 5). Chapter 4 of this book contains a discussion of this. For more on these campaigns see Drezner (2019).

Bibliography

Anton, Michael. The Trump Doctrine. April 20, 2019. *Foreign Policy*. Retrieved from https://foreignpolicy.com/2019/04/20/the-trump-doctrine-big-think-america-first-nationalism/.

Blackwill, Robert D. Trump's Foreign Policies Are Better than They Seem. April 2019. *Council on Foreign Relations*. Retrieved from https://www.cfr.org/report/trumps-foreign-policies-are-better-they-seem.

Brands, Hal. U.S. Grand Strategy in an Age of Nationalism: Fortress America and Its Alternatives. 2017a. *The Washington Quarterly*, 40(1): 73–94.

Brands, Hal. The Unexceptional Superpower: American Grand Strategy in the Age of Trump. 2017b. *Survival*, 59(6): 7–40.

Brands, Hal. *American Grand Strategy in the Age of Trump*. Washington, DC: Brookings Institution Press, 2018.

Brooks, Stephen, and William Wohlforth. The Rise and Fall of the Great Powers in the Twenty-first Century: China's Rise and the Fate of America's Global Position. 2015/2016. *International Security*, 40(3): 7–53.

Daalder, Ivo H., and James M. Lindsay. *The Empty Throne: America's Abdication of Global Leadership*. New York: Public Affairs, 2018.

Drezner, Daniel W. Economic Statecraft in the Age of Trump. 2019. *The Washington Quarterly*, 42(3): 7–24.

Dueck, Colin. Tillerson the Realist. January 16, 2017. *Foreign Policy Research Institute*. Retrieved from www.fpri.org/article/2017/01/tillerson-the-realist/.

Dueck, Colin. *Age of Iron: On Conservative Nationalism*. New York: Oxford University Press, 2019.

Edwards, Jason A. Make America Great Again: Donald Trump and Redefining the U.S. Role in the World. 2018. *Communication Quarterly*, 66(2): 176–195.

Friedman, George. Donald Trump Has a Coherent, Radical Foreign Policy Doctrine. January 20, 2017. *RealClearWorld*. Retrieved from https://www.realclearworld.com/articles/2017/01/20/donald_trump_has_a_coherent_radical_foreign_policy_doctrine_112180.html.

Friedman, George. The Trump Doctrine. July 11, 2018. *Geopolitical Futures*. Retrieved from https://geopoliticalfutures.com/the-trump-doctrine/.

Glasser, John, Christopher A. Preble, and A. Trevor Thrall. *Fuel to the Fire: How Trump Made America's Broken Foreign Policy Even Worse (and How We Can Recover)*. Washington, DC: CATO Institute, 2019.

Goldberg, Jeffrey. The Obama Doctrine. April 2016. *The Atlantic*. Retrieved from https://www.theatlantic.com/magazine/archive/2016/04/the-obama-doctrine/471525/.

Goldberg, Jeffrey. A Senior White House Official Defines the Trump Doctrine: 'We're America, Bitch'. June 11, 2018. *The Atlantic*. Retrieved from https://www.theatlantic.com/politics/archive/2018/06/a-senior-white-house-official-defines-the-trump-doctrine-were-america-bitch/562511/.

Goldgeier, James. The Misunderstood Roots of International Order – And Why They Matter Again. 2018. *The Washington Quarterly*, 41(3): 7–20.

Herbert, Jon, Trevor McCrisken, and Andrew Wroe (eds.). *The Ordinary Presidency of Donald J. Trump*. Cham, Switzerland: Palgrave Macmillan, 2019.

Herman, Arthur. The Trump Doctrine: American Interests Come First. December 19, 2017. *The Hudson Institute*. Retrieved from https://www.hudson.org/research/14073-the-trump-doctrine-american-interests-come-first.

Hoover, Amanda. Why Henry Kissinger is Optimistic about Trump and His Policies. December 20, 2016. *The Christian Science Monitor*. Retrieved from https://www.csmonitor.com/USA/2016/1220/Why-Henry-Kissinger-is-optimistic-about-Trump-and-his-policies.

Huxley, Tim, and Benjamin Schreer. Trump's Missing Asia Strategy. 2017. *Survival*, 59(3): 81–89.

Ikenberry, John G. The End of Liberal International Order? January 2018. International Affairs, 94(1): 7–23.

Jervis, Robert. Do Leaders Matter and How Would We Know? May 2013. *Security Studies*, 22(2): 153–179.

Jervis, Robert. President Trump and International Relations Theory. In (eds.) Jervis, Robert, et al. *Chaos in the Liberal Order: The Trump Presidency and International Politics in the Twenty-First Century*. New York: Columbia University Press, 2018.

Kaine, Tim. A New Truman Doctrine: Grand Strategy in a Hyperconnected World. 2017. *Foreign Affairs*, 96(4): 36–53.

Larres, Klaus. Donald Trump and America's Grand Strategy: US Foreign Policy toward Europe, Russia and China. May 2017. *Global Policy*. Retrieved from https://archive.transatlanticrelations.org/wp-content/uploads/2017/05/Larres-Donald-Trump-and-America%E2%80%99s-Grand-Strategy-U.S.-foreign-policy-toward-Europe-Russia-and-China-Global-Policy-May-2017.pdf.

Layne, Christopher. The Big Forces of History. January/February 2017. *American Conservative*. Retrieved from https://www.theamericanconservative.com/articles/the-big-forces-of-history/.

Lissner, Rebecca Friedman, and Mira Rapp-Hooper. The Day after Trump: American Strategy for a New International Order. 2018. *The Washington Quarterly*, 41(1): 7–25.

Manning, Bayless. The Congress, the Executive and Intermestic Affairs: Three Proposals. 1977. *Foreign Affairs*, 55(2): 306–324.

Mazarr, Michael J. Preserving the Post-War Order. 2017. *The Washington Quarterly*, 40(2): 2017: 29–49.

Mazarr, Michael J., Timothy R. Heath, and Astrid Stuth Cevallos. China and the International Order. 2018. *RAND*. Retrieved from https://www.rand.org/content/dam/rand/pubs/research_reports/RR2400/RR2423/RAND_RR2423.pdf (accessed November 20, 2018).

Mearsheimer, John J. Donald Trump Should Embrace a Realist Foreign Policy. November 27, 2016. *The National Interest*. Retrieved from https://nationalinterest.org/feature/donald-trump-should-embrace-realist-foreign-policy-18502.

Norrlof, Carla. Hegemony and Inequality: Trump and the Liberal Playbook. 2018. International Affairs, 94(1): 63–88.

Ordonez, Franco. Morale Disintegrates at State Department as Diplomats Wonder Who Will Quit Next to Escape Trump. January 13, 2018. *McClatchy*. Retrieved from https://www.mcclatchydc.com/news/politics-government/white-house/article194607714.html.

Powaski, Ronald E. *Ideals, Interests, and U.S. Foreign Policy from George H.W. Bush to Donald Trump*. Cham, Switzerland: Palgrave Macmillan, 2019.

Rathbun, Brian. Does Structure Trump All? A Test of Agency in World Politics. In (eds.) Jervis, Robert, et al. *Chaos in the Liberal Order: The Trump Presidency and International Politics in the Twenty-First Century*. New York: Columbia University Press, 2018.

Rovere, Crispin. Donald Trump, a Nixon-Kissinger realist (part 1). April 7, 2016. *Lowy Institute*. Retrieved from https://www.lowyinstitute.org/the-interpreter/donald-trump-nixon-kissinger-realist-part-1.

Sanger, David E., and Maggie Haberman. 50 G.O.P. Officials Warn Donald Trump Would Put Nation's Security 'at Risk'. August 8, 2016. *New York Times*. Retrieved from https://www.nytimes.com/2016/08/09/us/politics/national-security-gop-donald-trump.html (accessed November 20, 2018).

Schweller, Randall. Opposite but Compatible Nationalisms: A Neoclassical Realist Approach to the Future of US–China Relations. Spring 2018a. *Chinese Journal of International Politics*, 11(1): 23–48.

Schweller, Randall L. Why Trump Now: A Third–Image Explanation. In (eds.) Jervis, Robert, et al. *Chaos in the Liberal Order: The Trump Presidency and International Politics in the Twenty-First Century*. New York: Columbia University Press, 2018b.

Schweller, Randall. Three Cheers for Trump's Foreign Policy. What the Establishment Misses. September/October 2018c. *Foreign Affairs*, 97(5): 133–143.

Stokes, Doug. Trump, American Hegemony and the Future of the Liberal International Order. 2018. International Affairs, 94(1): 133–150.

Sullivan, Jake. The World After Trump: How the System Can Endure. 2018. *Foreign Affairs*, 97(2): 1–9.

Trump, Donald. Full text: Trump's 2017 U.N. speech transcript. September 19, 2017. *Politico*. Retrieved from https://www.politico.com/story/2017/09/19/trump-un-speech-2017-full-text-transcript-242879.

Walt, Stephen. No, Donald Trump is Not a Realist. April 1, 2016. *Foreign Policy*. Retrieved from http://foreignpolicy.com/2016/04/01/norealdonaldtrump-is-not-a-realist/.

Walt, Stephen. This isn't Realpolitik. This is Amateur Hour. May 3, 2017. *Foreign Policy*. Retrieved from https://foreignpolicy.com/2017/05/03/this-isnt-realpolitik-this-is-amateur-hour/.

Waltz, Kenneth. *Man, the State, and War*. New York: Columbia University Press, 1954.

War on the Rocks. Open Letter on Donald Trump from GOP National Security Leaders. March 2, 2016. Retrieved from https://warontherocks.com/2016/03/open-letter-on-donald-trump-from-gop-national-security-leaders/.

White House. Remarks by President Trump on the Administration's National Security Strategy. December 18, 2017. Retrieved from https://www.whitehouse.gov/briefings-statements/remarks-president-trump-administrations-national-security-strategy/.

Wohlforth, William C. Unipolarity, Status Competition, and Great Power War. In (ed.) John Ikenberry. *International Relations Theory and the Consequences of Unipolarity*. Cambridge: Cambridge University Press, 2011.

2 Trump, the agent of change and domestic drivers of US foreign policy

Introduction

This chapter outlines a number of key aspects of Donald J. Trump's personality and behavior, and domestic factors that informed the foreign policy positions he adopted during the 2016 presidential campaign. His operating style guided not just the methods he used throughout the campaign, but has continued to influence the administration's tactics, methods, and strategy since the advent of his presidency (Chapters 3 and 4 discuss this in more detail). The chapter contains three sections. The first considers the president's tactics during the 2016 US presidential election, making the case that candidate Trump, as well as his campaign, pursued his objectives with doggedness and made a number of adroit decisions. This suggests his behavior is more rational – in terms of achieving his ends – than his critics are often willing to recognize. Section two uses the *individual level* of analysis. It draws attention to President Trump as a key actor and agent of US foreign policy. Since the 1980s, Donald J. Trump has espoused a consistent set of views on foreign policy, including the idea that America's friends, partners, and adversaries were exploiting the US, necessitating major adjustments in US foreign policy. This state of affairs was – in Trump's view – the product of the incompetent leadership of a class of misguided and ineffective elites in Washington. To correct this, he argued he could use the unique deal-making skills he obtained during his business career and personal 'genius' to enact change. All the while, he displays a commitment to utilizing lies, deception, and misdirection to achieve his ends. This is married to a ruthless, transactional view of social behavior acquired throughout his life – a view he believes is reflected in the self-interested behavior of states in the international arena. As such, he has rejected America's self-ordained 'exceptionalism'. The third section shifts to the *domestic level* of analysis, identifying a number of domestic factors that Trump tapped into during the 2016 election and that influence his administration's foreign policy. This includes public opinion favorable to the president's stated desire to reduce America's global commitments; the legacy and political style of President Andrew Jackson (1829–1837), who acts as the philosophical inspiration for elements of Trump's foreign policy; and the emergence of a 'restraint constituency' in American politics.

The final section makes a case that, ultimately, given the larger than life personality of President Trump and the ruthless determination and deceptive methods he utilizes to pursue his ends, no consideration of his foreign policy can be divorced from the operating style and personal preferences outlined here. As we'll see in subsequent chapters, they continue to infuse the tactics, methods, and strategy of his foreign policy.

A method to the madness? The 2016 presidential election

Owing to his seemingly irrational and impulsive behavior it is easy to consider Trump's political success to be the product of luck, which certainly in some measure contributes to the success of any political campaign. Yet, it cannot be ignored that he has generally been successful at the tasks he has set himself throughout his life, whether it was to acquire wealth and fame during his pre-presidential career or to secure the presidency in 2016. To assume Trump's victory was a fluke misreads a number of key decisions he made during the 2016 campaign. For example, his strategy focused on seizing the formerly industrialized 'rustbelt' states (Indiana, Michigan, Ohio, Wisconsin, and Pennsylvania) from the Democratic Party as the path to winning the Electoral College (Silver, 2017). This looked like a risky strategy, as these states were viewed as part of Hillary Clinton's vaunted 'blue firewall' (states that had voted for Democrats in 4 out of the prior 6 elections). Instead, political commentators and GOP strategists said Trump should target other 'battleground' states where he had a greater chance (according to the polls) of winning (Kirkland, 2016). Polls taken throughout the election campaign supported this notion, showing Trump trailing Clinton in Michigan and Wisconsin by up to seven percentage points, a seemingly insurmountable lead (Cassidy, 2016). But targeting the battleground states rather than the rustbelt states overlooked the fact that there was always a higher probability that some of the battleground states would tilt towards Trump; so with time running short it was imperative that he gamble and try to wrench the rustbelt states out of Clinton's firewall, without which he could not win the election *even if* he did win the battleground states. In other words, it was absolutely strategically the right move for Trump to target the rustbelt. He engaged this strategy by choosing to campaign across the rustbelt in the final weeks of the race (Smith and Kreutz, 2016). Moreover, the economies of these states, once home to America's formidable steel industry, had been devastated by economic change and globalized economies in recent decades. Trump's campaign understood that the memories, sometimes highly romanticized, held by the citizens of these states of a more affluent and hopeful past made them especially susceptible to a message that Trump would bring jobs back to the American working class. This was embodied in the slogan, 'Make America Great *Again*'.

Trump's choice of personnel and determination to cycle through senior campaign advisors depending upon his political fortunes were also effective. His decision to fire Corey Lewandowski as his Campaign Manager on June 20, 2016, and replace him with Paul Manafort came during a period of decline in the polls. Trump's position in the polls improved shortly thereafter (RealClearPolitics, 2016). Then, on August 17, 2016, his campaign announced that long-time Republican campaign manager and pollster, Kellyanne Conway, was being promoted from Senior Advisor to Campaign Manager, while Executive Chair of Breitbart News, Steve Bannon, would be brought on board as Campaign Chief Executive to replace Paul Manafort. The Bannon–Conway tandem seemed the oddest of pairings, and one destined to generate dysfunction at the highest levels of Trump's campaign given their disparate backgrounds: Conway was widely respected across the Republican establishment – parts of which aggressively opposed Trump's candidacy – as a professional and measured operator; Bannon, on the other hand, was an outsider and champion of the 'alt-right', a movement that embraces American (often white) nationalism, rejects mainstream conservativism, opposes immigration, multiculturalism, and political correctness. Yet, this shakeup occurred precisely when it was called for. It followed another period of weak polls for the Trump campaign in early August 2016 where Trump fell 7–8% behind Hillary Clinton's polling average (RealClearPolitics, 2016). After the rearrangement of senior personnel in his campaign, Trump's chance of success would never reach such a low point again.

Bringing Bannon and Conway on board had the effect of shoring up Trump's position and sharpened his campaign messaging, allowing Trump-leaning voters to see in his behavior what they wanted to see. This was evident during his sudden and surprising trip to Mexico on August 31, 2016, to meet and hold a press conference with Mexican President Enrique Peña Nieto (Gajanan, 2016). Prior to this, Trump had heavily and emotively criticized Mexico for allowing migrants of questionable character to cross the border (Time, 2015). Despite this rhetoric, Trump was calm during the press conference, leading some to suggest that Conway was making real progress in restraining his behavior. However, Trump followed his subdued trip to Mexico by delivering a raucous immigration speech to his followers in Arizona on the same night, during which he reaffirmed his hard-line immigration policy and declared that Mexico would pay for a wall along the US–Mexico border. This had all the hallmarks of Bannon's influence. In the space of a single day Trump had made an unprecedented trip to Mexico where he acted with moderation, showing that he was capable of looking presidential to moderate Republican voters hesitant of voting for him, and also showed his base of diehard fans at his Arizona rally that he was not abandoning his core hard-line immigration policy. Trump would utilize this contradictory approach over and over again throughout the campaign to great effect, reassuring both his moderate and hard-line supporters that he remained committed to them even if his behavior was, at other times, contradictory.

Scott Adams colorfully explained throughout the 2016 election how Trump adeptly used emotional persuasion (Adams, 2017; Goldhill, 2017). Cataloguing the rhetorical 'tit for tat' between Trump and his opponents, Adams argued that what appeared to be absurd statements often had a logic behind them. Consider the labeling of his political opponents. Marco Rubio was dubbed 'little Marco'; Jeb Bush became 'low energy Jeb'; Ted Cruz, 'lying Ted', and Hillary Clinton, 'crooked Hillary'. In doing so, Trump used a simple method to target opponents' weaknesses that played to voters' cognitive biases. For example, Jeb Bush was a relatively mild-mannered individual, akin to a rational chief executive officer (CEO) who would not be easily flustered during crises; surely a candidate US citizens might view as a credible future president. What should have been a political advantage turned into a liability after Trump labeled Bush 'low energy Jeb'. At a glance, Jeb Bush *did* look like a man devoid of excitement, charisma, or energy with no hope of matching the high energy of Trump. The same labeling tactic was evident when Trump called Hillary Clinton 'crooked Hillary'. By labeling Hillary as a 'crook' for months on end – a person who is dishonest or criminal – it primed voters to see her this way at a time when an email controversy was dogging the Clinton campaign and questions were being asked about the activities of the Clinton Foundation. Once the label was used, it created a "confirmation bias trap" (Taranto, 2016). No candidate except Trump had such an excellent grasp of these tactics.

A third key member of Trump's team was his son-in-law, Jared Kushner, who harnessed social media to the campaign's advantage. Kushner and his digital team utilized low-tech policy videos that garnered 74 million hits (Bertoni, 2016), micro-targeting inundated Trump-leaning voters with his blunt messaging and enabling the campaign to sell hats and t-shirts with Trump's 'Make American Great Again' slogan, turning people into human billboards (Ibid.). Trump's campaign expenditure is a testament to this, as spending on traditional television and online advertising was marginalized in favor of using Twitter and Facebook to drive the campaign, to get the message out and monitor the shifting mood of voter sentiment (Ibid.). Trump's Federal Election Commission filings through to mid-October showed that he only spent half as much as Clinton's campaign, revealing the dividends from this unorthodox approach (Ibid.). Again, a number of voices called this approach untested and likely to fail in the face of the Clinton campaign's formidable "get out the vote" infrastructure (Shepard, 2016). Brad Parscale, the leader of Trump's data hub, explained that the data operation was used to decide "every campaign decision: travel, fundraising, advertising, rally locations – even the topics of the speeches", and Kushner "put all the different pieces together. And what's funny is the outside world was so obsessed about this little piece or that, they didn't pick up that it was all being orchestrated so well" (Bertoni, 2016). Additionally, in January 2020 Facebook's Vice President Andrew Bosworth, responding to the question of whether Facebook was responsible for Trump's election, said "I think the answer is yes, but not for the reasons anyone thinks. He didn't get elected because of Russia or misinformation or Cambridge Analytica. He got elected because he ran the single best digital ad campaign I've ever seen from any advertiser. Period ... The use of custom audiences, video, ecommerce, and fresh creative remains the high water mark of digital ad campaigns in my opinion" (Bosworth, 2020).

Ultimately the core of Trump's team was Trump. The bombastic nature of his rhetoric escalated from day to day, week to week, and debate to debate, and his key policy planks played upon people's fears while differentiating him from the rest of his Republican rivals (Coleman, 2019).[1] It came to the point where no single outrageous thing Trump said, and which would have been a campaign killer for any normal candidate, had much of an impact. Trump, by disregarding all traditional norms of political behavior and political correctness, shifted the public's sense of what was acceptable for a politician to say. This arguably desensitized the public, all the while generating headlines that kept him on the front pages of every newspaper in America and giving his speeches prime time coverage on cable news networks (Georgantopoulos, 2016).

Indeed, candidate Trump displayed an uncanny understanding of how to gain the attention of the US media. A study from Harvard's Kennedy School of Government showed that throughout 2015 and in the lead-up to the Republican primaries, major news media directed a disproportionately high volume of coverage to Trump given his low polling numbers at the time (Patterson, 2016). Furthermore, Trump received more good press than bad, helping to elevate him to the top of Republican polls (Ibid.). Other analysts claim that the media coverage he received during the primaries corresponded to $2 billion in free advertising (Byers, 2016), and another study by the University of Wisconsin explained that "Trump proved himself uniquely able to satisfy the imperative of dominating the news agenda, entering the news cycle ... and repeatedly re-entering it, with stories and initiatives so that subsequent news coverage is set on your [Trump's] terms" (Wells, Shah, Pevehouse, Yang, Pelled, Boehm, et al., 2016, 670). Trump was possibly aided by the fact that a majority of the American populace no longer trusted the mainstream media, parts of which were critical of Trump, noting his penchant for lying, with a Gallup poll in September showing that only 32% of Americans trusted the media "to report the news fully, accurately and fairly", the lowest level on record in Gallup polling history (Swift, 2016). Trump's principle appeared to be that any exposure was good exposure, and he manipulated the public's thirst for outrage to his advantage unlike any political candidate in modern times.

In short, a case can be made that Trump made a number of rational decisions throughout the 2016 US election campaign that were obscured by his bellicosity and wild rhetoric. His often contradictory statements on a range of issues bewildered his opponents (and many mainstream political commentators), diverting attention away from the cunning moves he was making. Another way of viewing this is that Trump has a shameless Machiavellian streak that most people – even politicians willing to bend and distort the truth to achieve their ends – generally do not have.

Trump's foreign policy philosophy and personal characteristics

Long-held convictions

Authors such as Charlie Laderman, Brendan Simms, and Thomas Wright have considered statements Trump made over three decades by trawling through interviews, articles, books, and tweets (Laderman and Simms, 2017; Wright, 2016). They find that Trump consistently espoused a number of views since the late 1980 that amount to a foreign policy philosophy. This includes his long-standing assertion that the US is an international laughing stock that is exploited by its friends and allies (who are unwilling to pay their share for their own defense and should thus monetarily compensate the US for protecting them), that it is enmeshed in a range of unfair international trading arrangements and overcommitted internationally (requiring it to reduce its commitment to the existing international liberal order); his concern over immigration from Mexico; and opposition to international environment regulations that restrict US economic growth. Finally, for Trump there is always a major state beyond America's shores that stands out in terms of its unwillingness to play by the rules and that constitutes a primary adversary – in the 1980s it was Japan; by the 2000s, it would be China. Therefore, once in office, China was formally elevated to a peer competitor and a revisionist state challenging and seeking to displace America's global power – a threat that necessitated a response (discussed in Chapter 4).

Trump claimed that what the US expended abroad had come at the cost of reducing America's ability to invest in its own infrastructure, protect jobs, and raise military spending. Jason Edwards explains that Trump concluded that America's "globalist" post-Cold War foreign policy has, in Trump's own words, "veered badly off course", stretching US resources thin (Edwards, 2018, 181). Thus, Trump seeks to rationalize and discipline America's attention and resources. This involves rejecting efforts aimed at nation-building and "spreading universal values" (Ibid., 182) – an approach that conforms to Trump's understanding of the social world discussed below. Indeed, Trump channeled John Quincy Adams when he declared in April 2016 that the US should "not go abroad in search of enemies" (Ibid., 183). To Trump, the "globalist" policies of Obama and Hillary Clinton were a recipe for chaos that led the US to "lose control of its destiny" (Ibid., 182) – they made America reliant upon other states which had failed to fulfil their obligations. As such, Trump's "economic nationalist" creed is an effort to reassert domestic control over the economy and requires altering unfair international trading arrangements, withdrawing from multilateral regimes, and reducing immigration (Lissner and Rapp-Hooper, 2018, 17).

Trump directly linked his long-held positions and domestic agenda to the international system: Poor trade deals and 'unfair' trading arrangements had damaged the US working class and offshored US jobs; foreign actors had been elevated to existential threats, necessitating the costly and misguided use of American military power abroad; US allies relied on American power for their security, allowing them to keep their military budgets low while US tax payers had to fork out to protect them, which required the US to reconsider its commitments to allies and vaunted long-standing alliance pacts, such as NATO; Mexico sent its worst people to the US (a problem compounded by weak border policies from the US federal government), etc. This speaks to the fact that the march of globalization has, in some respects, collapsed the distinction between the domestic and international: An interconnected international system and economy breaks down borders and ensures that national fortune and state security are interconnected. Policies at home have to take this into account and, ultimately, it is much harder for states to be in control of their own domestic destiny. As such, Laderman and Simms note that "much of Trump's domestic programme depends on what he does abroad" (Laderman and Simms, 2017, 10), and that given the checks and balances that prevent most presidents from passing sweeping domestic legislation, "this means that the rest of the world will be much more exposed to a Trump presidency than Americans themselves" (Ibid.). It also suggested that from the outset of the Trump presidency the US would not become notably more isolationist. As Trump said: "I'm a nationalist and a globalist. I'm both. And I'm the only one who makes the decision" (Dueck, 2019, 133).

The work of Laderman and Simms makes clear that Trump came to the presidency with long-standing convictions on foreign policy and, therefore, he was "no mere opportunist" (Laderman and Simms, 2017, 8). As such, on election night Trump declared, "I really don't change my mind very much … go back and look, my position on trade has been solid for many, many years, since I was a very young person talking about how we were getting ripped off by the rest of the world" (Ibid., 123). Having come to power seeking to enact significant change in how the US engaged the world, Donald Trump no doubt took his victory to be a mandate to turn his policy preferences into reality – something the next section shows he felt uniquely suited to achieve.

Trump, the 'stable genius' and charismatic leader

In January 2018, President Trump tweeted: "throughout my life, my two greatest assets have been mental stability and being, like, really smart." In a following tweet he proclaimed himself to be "a very stable genius" (@realDonaldTrump, January 6, 2018). To Trump, virtually all of America's recent failures were the result of incompetent US elite leadership. As he closed in on the GOP presidential nomination he said that "foolishness and arrogance ... led to one foreign policy disaster after another" (Trump, 2016a), and if elected he would "look for talented experts with new approaches, and practical ideas", not "those who have perfect résumés but very little to brag about except responsibility for a long history of failed policies and continued losses at war" (Rovere, 2016). Trump certainly has immense belief in himself, declaring at the 2016 Republican convention: "I alone can fix it" (Laderman and Simms, 2017, 5). At other times he has stated that "I'm my own strategist"; that "People need ego, whole nations need ego. I think our country needs more ego" (Klein, 2016; Hartmann, 2017), and in response to questions about why senior official positions and ambassadorships in the State Department remained vacant after 10 months of his presidency he said it did not matter because, "I'm the only one that matters" (Chappell, 2017). These quotes indicate that President Trump considers himself to be at the apex of American power and the decisive agent of policy change. This likely contributes to his penchant for engaging in personal diplomacy vis-à-vis other world leaders; his view of himself as the most important actor in the US suggests he thinks the same applies in other countries so direct appeals, hastily arranged photo ops and joint press conferences with foreign leaders, and seeking leader–leader summits (bypassing traditional diplomatic processes) are legitimate and necessary steps to establishing ties with decisive actors in other nations to pursue US interests and secure deals.

Trump's self-styled genius leadership is a charismatic one. Under this kind of governance the "great transformation", as described by Taesuh Cha, is given coherence and a singular voice (Cha, 2017, 84).[2] Walter Russell Mead argues that for those inspired by a Jacksonian vision (the Jacksonian tradition of US foreign policy is discussed below) of leadership, this depends upon trust (Mead, 2017, 4). Trump cemented this by repeatedly claiming during his campaign that he was not owned by special interests, unlike his competitors, and therefore could tell the truth. For example in 2016 he said: "I am proudly not a politician, because I am not behold to any special interest, I've spent a lot of money on my campaign, I'll tell you. I write those checks. Nobody owns Trump" (Trump, 2016b).

And where trust exists, followers will accept policies even those that appear difficult to successfully implement (Mead, 2017, 4). This willingness to accept these policies is in keeping with charismatic leadership outlined by Weber who argued that charismatic leaders are "set apart from ordinary people and treated as endowed with supernatural, superhuman, or at least specifically exceptional powers or qualities" (Weber, 1947, 328). Hannah Arendt expanded on Weber's discussion of charismatic leadership, writing: "that modern society in its desperate inability to form judgements will take every individual for what he considers himself and professes himself to be ... Extraordinary self-confidence and displays of self-confidence therefore inspire confidence in others; pretensions to genius waken the conviction in others that they are indeed dealing with a genius" (Arendt quoted in Eatwell, 2006, 141–142). Trump sets himself apart from all others with inflated claims of intellect, vision, courage, and the like. His policies, foreign policies included, need not make rational sense, instead followers feel inspired by Trump's charisma and vision, and make an emotional commitment.

Steven Lukes argues that charismatic leaders are "exceptional and disruptive" (Lukes, 2017). The charismatic leader possesses unique capabilities. In 2013 Trump claimed his IQ to be higher than both Presidents Obama and George W. Bush (@realDonaldTrump, May 1, 2013). At the launch of his campaign in 2015 he described himself as a great leader saying the US "needs a truly great leader, and we need a truly great leader now. We need a leader that wrote 'The Art of the Deal'" (Time, 2015). Then, in 2016, he tweeted about his unique grasp of US tax laws, "I know our complex tax laws better than anyone who has ever run for president and am the only one who can fix them" (@realDonaldTrump, October 2, 2016). And soon after his presidential term commenced, he related his self-professed prowess to his understanding of US relations with NATO when, during a rally on April 12, 2016, in Rome, New York, he recounted being asked about his views on NATO. He noted that while he was not an expert he nonetheless claimed, "I'm smart, I'm like a smart person. So they asked me, I'm like a smart person" (Factbase, 2016). And just days earlier Trump proclaimed himself and his views on NATO vindicated when it was reported that NATO Secretary General Jens Stoltenberg was criticized in a closed-door meeting by US Senators for failing to get promised funding from member countries (Hudson, 2016). Trump tweeted, "Looks like I was right about NATO. I had no doubt" (@realDonaldTrump, April 8, 2016).

Trump also sees himself as the man to remake US trade relationships. In May 2014, he tweeted that the American worker was being treated badly and that "We need smart trade which can only be accomplished by smart dealmakers" (@realDonaldTrump, May 30, 2014). As he campaigned against passage of the Trans Pacific Partnership (TPP) he repeatedly called for 'smart' trade and suggested that he was the person to deliver it. The trade deficit with China, and concerns over intellectual property, resulted from 'stupid' trade negotiations undertaken by his predecessors. 'Stupid' trade and 'stupid' trade negotiators was a theme he repeated time and again. To underscore this point he tweeted in 2018, "The U.S. has made such bad trade deals over so many years that we can only WIN!" (@realDonaldTrump, June 4, 2018). Trump justified the use of tariffs as leverage in negotiations over US–China trade saying "I happen to be a tariff person because I'm a smart person, OK?" (Wall Street Journal, 2018). All of this was tied to his supposedly unique expertise as he declared "[I] Know the Chinese", because he understood "the Chinese mind" owing to his dealings with Chinese businesses (Laderman and Simms, 2017, 83–84). In short, from Trump's viewpoint none of the goals articulated during the campaign would or could be brought to successful fruition without his unique insight and skill.

Transaction man and the end of US exceptionalism

Despite his long-held convictions on major aspects of US foreign policy, the president does not appear to have a coherent political ideology: Historically, he has run for the presidency as an independent, been a registered Democrat and a Republican, and donated to politicians of both parties (Gillin, 2015). Statements by individuals that have spent hundreds of hours with Trump during his business career reinforce the notion that the president is ideologically ambivalent on both a personal and professional level. For example, Tony Schwartz (co-writer with Trump of *The Art of the Deal*) said that he thought Trump was "value-free", had "no conscience" and "He doesn't make a distinction between right and wrong" (Netflix, 2018). To Trump, the world of both personal and international relations is fundamentally Darwinian. In this, Schwartz said: "He [Trump] has a very primitive world view, a very binary world view, which I believe came from his relationship with his father" (Ibid.). Trump also said in a 1980 interview that life is "combat" and an endless struggle for victory where no one can be trusted in a world of "killers" (Laderman and Simms, 2017, 5). In Trump's words, people's "motivation is rarely what it seems to be, and it's almost never pure altruism" (Trump and Schwartz, 2015 edition, 367). Indeed, apparently on ski trips with his children he would jab at them with a pole to get ahead of them and he told them, "Don't trust anyone", testing them by asking whether they trusted him and chastising them if they said they did (Coppins, 2019). In another account he said, "Watch out for people", "even [those] close to you, because in the end, if it's a choice between you and them, they're usually going to choose themselves ... Sad, isn't it? You really have to think of yourself as a one-man show ... So don't expect anyone to be on your side" (Shell, 2019, 40). To Trump, self-interest is the fundamental driver of human behavior – including in the international domain. In 1990 when asked how a future President Trump would approach foreign policy he said: "He [Trump] would believe very strongly in extreme military strength. He wouldn't trust anyone" (Plaskin, 1990).

The president's ideological ambivalence offers an *individual-level* explanation for his rejection of US 'exceptionalism' – the idea that the US is somehow unique (and even superior) among the world's nations and has a moral mission to spread its 'universal' values abroad and promote a liberal international order.[3] The exceptionalist sentiment gels with the liberal school of political thought in the United States. The liberal impulse here works in two ways: On one hand it can *prevent* US action abroad by asserting that a moral threshold be reached for action to take place – this can limit US cooperation with illiberal states or prevent it from seizing the strategic initiative for material gain when opportunities present themselves. Trump has a history of saying that while he disagreed with the invasion of Iraq in 2003 (although he also supported it at other times), since the US did invade, it should "take the oil ... It's not stealing, we're reimbursing ourselves" (Borger, 2016). Although this objective is at odds with international law, Trump affirmed in November 2019 this as the key rationale for keeping US forces in eastern Syria (Borger, 2019).

At other times, a sense of moralism may *compel* behavior to change the world in the US image or to address humanitarian emergencies; steps that may backfire on the US strategically and destabilize countries and regions despite America's good intentions (Walt, 2018; Mearsheimer, 2018). Trump's first Secretary of State, Rex Tillerson, briefly touched upon the rationale behind the administration's approach, explaining that the administration was de-emphasizing human rights concerns as it created "obstacles to our ability to advance our national security interests, our economic interests" (Borger, 2017). While some US administrations have relegated the role that American values and American exceptionalism should play in US foreign policy relative to America's material interests, they have usually paid some lip-service to the importance of US values and its example as a democracy that gives hope for the oppressed worldwide. But Trump, more than perhaps any US president before him, has gone out of his way to reject American exceptionalism and thus the role he thinks US values should play in foreign policy. For example US budget director, Mick Mulvaney, made a telling point when he announced the administration's first budget, which increased military spending and reduced the State Department's budget by 28%, stating, "This is a *hard-power budget*, and that was done intentionally. The president very clearly wants to send a message to our allies and to our potential adversaries that this is a strong-power administration" (Berman, 2016). And in February 2017 with then-Fox News host, Bill O'Reilly, Trump, after saying he respected Russian President Vladimir Putin, was asked why when "he's [Putin] a killer". Trump established moral equivalency between Washington and Moscow, saying "There are a lot of killers. You think our country's so innocent?" (Tatum, 2017). And in the context of discussing trade he named Russia and China as foes, but also added "that doesn't mean they are bad. It doesn't mean anything. It means that they are competitive" (Contiguglia, 2018). Finally, Freedom House reported in 2018 that "Even when he chose to acknowledge America's treaty alliances with fellow democracies, the president spoke of cultural or civilizational ties rather than shared recognition of universal rights ... Indeed, the American leader expressed feelings of admiration and even personal friendship for some of the world's most loathsome strongmen and dictators" (Freedom House, 2018).

Rather than an impediment to US action, Stephen Wertheim writes that Trump's rejection of American exceptionalism and liberal values as guides to US behavior is viewed as an enabler of action, stating "Trump rejects exceptionalism less because it insults others than because he thinks it paralyzes the United States. It prevents America from throwing itself into the game of international relations, or international deal-making, and playing to win. In thrall to exceptionalism, Americans tolerate, even welcome, mutual gains and shared prosperity, so long as they imagine themselves as blazing the path to freedom" (Wertheim, 2018, 129). To Trump, ideology and exceptionalism are irrelevant in this process. On this topic Colin Dueck writes that there is no evidence that Trump "is utterly fixed upon dismantling rules-based liberal international order, any more than on upholding it. Rather, he looks to pull existing arrangements in the direction of what he views as material US interests, and is open to either renegotiating or abandoning those arrangements case by case" (Dueck, 2019, 132). In short, to Trump and key actors in his administration, US exceptionalism restricts action when it may be wise and compels hasty actions that undermine the national interest, and every state, whether friend, ally or enemy, should overtly work to benefit US interests. This is the metric (determined by Trump himself) upon which the US would decide to assist or work productively with another country. Alluding to this when answering a question about when the US would intervene to help a state in the time of a humanitarian crisis, Trump said "it depends on the country, the region, how friendly they've been to us" (Daalder and Lindsay, 2018, 34). And Rosa Brooks suggested just prior to Trump's victory: "To Trump, U.S. alliances, like potential business partners in a real estate transaction, should always be asked: 'What have you done for me lately?'" (Brooks, 2016).

The path to reaching favorable deals for the US requires, in Trump's mind, an almost wholly transactional view of the world; one in which the US must be the toughest in order to 'win' and get the most out of any negotiation with foreign partners. To Trump, "tough is winning systematically" (Laderman and Simms, 2017, 48). As such, Ivo Daalder and James M. Lindsay explain that "When Trump surveyed the world, he saw only competitors ... he would judge them not on sentimentalities about the past but on their willingness to make deals that he liked" (2018, 6). And just days before he took the oath of office he said "So, I give everybody an even start ... Right now, as far as I'm concerned, everybody's got an even start" (Ibid., 6). Additionally, former Trump officials H.R. McMaster (Former United States National Security Advisor) and Gary D. Cohn (Chief Economic Advisor) wrote in May 2017 in the *Wall Street Journal* that "Simply put, America will treat others as they treat us ... Where our interests align, we are open to working together to solve problems and explore opportunities" (McMaster and Cohn, 2017).

Trump's reference to an 'even start' did not suggest America's partners would receive equal outcomes as a result of engaging or making deals with the US. On this, Trump has earlier said: "You hear lots of people say that a great deal is when both sides win. That is a bunch of crap. In a great deal you win – not the other side. You crush the opponent and come away with *something better* for yourself" (Daalder and Lindsay, 2018, 8). Taking advantage of others is morally legitimate in Trump's worldview. Speaking alongside Chinese President Xi Jinping about how China had been 'exploiting' the US, he said "I don't blame China ... After all, who can blame a country for being able to take advantage of another country for the benefit of its citizens? I give China great credit" (Vitali, 2017). Trump also spoke glowingly of Ronald Reagan (Kaczynski, 2015). To Trump, Reagan's success had nothing to do with luck but stemmed from the fact he "believed in toughing it out, even when under fire from his critics. He has the nerve to craft his policies toward dominance, always with his eye out for the right deal" (Ibid.). Undoubtedly, Trump believes his own toughness and deal-making prowess equate him with Reagan and will allow him to secure significant compacts during his presidential tenure.

Trump the deceiver[4]

Trump is adept at manipulation and persuasion (Adams, 2017), uses unconventional "linguistic devices" and language that, on one hand, contains emotive appeal (Nunn, 2016; Savoy, 2018) and on the other constructs a political identity that his supporters find authentic (Sclafani, 2018). Indeed history, as well as contemporary politics, reveals that for some political actors acquiring power over others is an almost maniacal driver and any means – lying, illegality, "dirty tricks", and falsification of the truth – should be borne to acquire it (Netflix, 2017; Guinote, 2017; Shirer, 1964). Trump's constant asser-tion that major US news outlets are 'fake media' and his more than 16,241 (!) false or misleading claims since the start of his presidency attest to the continued use of these tactics (Kessler, Rizzo, and Kelly, 2020). While deception has long been a tactic of politicians, Trump appears unique among leaders in modern liberal democracies in how often, openly and brazenly he uses it. This accords with Michael Pocalyko's claim that "Trump has embraced what Theodore Roosevelt called the 'bully pulpit' of the presidency, as well as char-acteristics that historian James MacGregor Burns admiringly ascribed to Franklin D. Roosevelt: the 'other side' of 'moral leadership', his 'shiftiness, his compromises, his manipulations'" (Pocalyko, 2017; Heisbourg, 2017). John Schuessler writes that "it would be going too far to suggest that there is no method to Trump's madness. It is just a different method … and while some US presidents used deception to forestall debate, to minimize controversy. The goal was to achieve broad support for their policies" (Schuessler, 2018, 376). By contrast, Trump and his surrogates welcome rhetorical combat with opposing elites. This, in turn, is taken as a sign by Trump's supporters that he is on "*their* side" (Ibid.).

Trump is comfortable with being surrounded by chaos. The portrait photographer Platon Antoniou recounts a telling story:

> I worked with Donald Trump quite a while ago, but even back then, there was this chaos and madness that surrounded him. I remember saying to him: 'Donald, how do you weather the storm? It's madness around you wherever you go, whatever you do, whatever you say. There's this sort of frenetic energy'. Suddenly,

this quiet calm came over him, and he said, 'I am the storm'. All this sort of frenetic, crazy energy and sense of chaos is very easy for Donald to navigate through that, because he created it. And it's actually us that can't cope with it.

(PBS, 2017)

Trump's approach to domestic governance and to international affairs – especially in terms of his rhetoric and messaging strategy – shows he is not just comfortable operating amidst chaos but actively promotes it. This overlaps with his opposition to acting predictably, a tactic addressed in the next chapter. Linked to this, Trump said "never let anyone know exactly where you're coming from. Knowledge is power, so keep as much of it to yourself as possible" (Kogan, 2019, 70). Finally, upon becoming president, Trump said in a television interview: "I just don't want people to know what my thinking is" (Ibid.).

Domestic drivers

Public opinion and the restraint agenda

Public opinion was conducive to aspects of the foreign policy agenda the president put forward during the 2016 election campaign. For example, in 2013, one survey by the Pew Research Center (PRC) showed 52% of Americans agreed with the statement that the US should "mind its own business internationally and let other countries get along the best they can on their own" (Brands, 2018, 76). Additional PRC polls in 2016 found 57% of Americans wanted Washington to "deal with its own problems and let others deal with theirs the best they can" while the majority of both Republicans and Democrats wanted Trump as president-elect to focus on domestic affairs, rather than on foreign policy (Pew Research Center, 2016). Polls also showed that Americans believed that the wars in Iraq and Afghanistan had not been worth it (Igielnik and Parker, 2019). These sentiments meshed with candidate Trump's promise to reduce America's international commitments.

Hal Brands, however, has noted that this 'isolationist' leaning was mitigated by the fact that 65% of Americans saw globalization as "mostly good" for the United States; 64% saw international trade as "good for their own standard of living"; 77% viewed NATO membership positively; and 89% agreed that sustaining U.S. alliances was "very or somewhat effective at achieving U.S. foreign policy goals" (Brands, 2018, 87). Despite this, throughout the 2015–2016 Republican and Democratic primaries, and then the presidential campaign, Americans backed candidates who questioned US post-Cold War strategy, with the eventual Democratic nominee Hillary Clinton being compelled to state she would not join the TPP, despite initially being a proponent of it during her tenure as Secretary of State (2009 to 2013). Furthermore, it is notable that Trump's predecessor, Barack Obama, also successfully ran for president on a platform that called for the US to reduce its foreign commitments, and especially its military footprint in the Middle East (Armbruster, 2011; Gerges, 2013). Indeed, Obama initially came to political prominence in 2002 by speaking out against the Bush administration's preparations for war against Iraq. Thus, Trump's assertion that US leaders had mishandled the invasion and occupation of Iraq likely resonated with anti-interventionist sections of the US electorate.

The 2016 election also tapped into the ideas of the 'restraint constituency' in American politics that opposes the pursuit of a grand strategy of liberal hegemony (Gholz, Press, and Sapolsky, 1997; Posen, 2014; Clarke and Ricketts, 2017). Its core argument is that this strategy, from Clinton to President Obama, has led the US to overreach through enunciation of ever-more ambitious foreign policy objectives. These have included: acquiring and sustaining a position of overwhelming military strength to dissuade and deter potential challengers; expansion of NATO into states formerly part of the Warsaw Pact and the Soviet Union; a strategy to expand the number of liberal democracies and promote Western values, declared "democratic enlargement" by the Clinton administration (Lake, 1993) in the belief that illiberal and rogue states threaten the US but democracies do not go to war with one another (Brown, Lynn-Jones, and Miller, 1996); and then the militarization of democratic enlargement during the Bush administration, leading to the immensely costly invasion of Iraq in 2003.

Advocates of restraint charge that not only has the strategy of liberal hegemony been extremely costly and thus self-defeating, but will become even less effective as the US power advantage declines relative to the rest of the world, and especially China. The cost of sustaining America's global footprint will require an ever greater outlay to sustain its position in the face of its competitors' growing capabilities. Additionally, it naturally induces states to balance the US, while US allies are able to 'free ride' on the back of America's power rather than carry their own weight and generate capabilities to defend themselves. Liberal hegemony is also unrealistically idealistic: It assumes US liberal values are globally applicable when, in fact, reactionary, nationalist, ethnic, and religious forces obstruct US objectives.

According to the restraint constituency the alternative to liberal hegemony is for the US to retrench its power and adopt a strategy of selective engagement and offshore balancing (Mearsheimer and Walt, 2016). The strategy is reformist; not revolutionary – it requires an incremental and staged reduction of US global military commitments, and US allies to do more as the US retrenches. A gradual approach will ensure rapid power vacuums do not emerge, and the US will have time to scale up its power in key regions should a regional or Eurasian hegemon emerge. In Europe, NATO should be adjusted and European states tasked with carrying more of their own security burden; in East Asia, the most difficult region in which to implement restraint owing to China's rise (and territorial tensions over the South China Seas with many of its neighbors), the US should sustain its security alliance with Japan, while Japan and South Korea should be compelled to do more; and in the Middle East the US should reduce its ground forces (which act as a source of recruitment for extremists) and resist the temptation to intervene in civil wars (as the US has little hope of getting the outcome it wants and, at worst, risks making matters worse). In other words, the US should 'offshore balance' against the possibility of a regional Middle Eastern hegemon emerging (Ibid.) and have commitments sufficient to ensure the continued flow of oil.

The return of the Jacksonian tradition

The philosophical wellspring of Trump's foreign policy lies in the populist presidency of Andrew Jackson (1829–1837) (Cha and Seo, 2018). Taesuh Cha explains that "the Trump ascendancy is no fluke. Indeed, it is embedded in the long history of political struggles between the liberal internationalism of the intellectual elite in metropolitan areas and the Jacksonian tradition of common Americans in rural communities" (Ibid., 83). Trump's populism and specific appeal to segments of the American electorate also align with Jackson's domestic political tactics, as it portrays and constructs "a folk community bound together by deep cultural and ethnic ties" in opposition to the liberal elites in the coastal areas, and upholds "a strong sense of White identity and violent hostility to other races" (Ibid.). To his supporters Trump's rhetoric is purportedly uplifting, containing "love for the homeland, fear of the foreigner, and righteous anger against corrupt elites who have endangered the nation's well-being" (Levinger, 2017, 1). Furthermore, in contrast to the 'corrupt' liberal coastal elites, Trump political base lies in non-urban areas where people prefer a greater level of foreign policy isolationism (Cha and Seo, 2018) and have less commitment than liberal elites to the mission of spreading US values around the world.

Largely absent from US grand strategy since World War II, Trump's appeal is, according to Mead, part of a populist "Jacksonian revolt" (Mead, 2017). Trump's marketing campaign of 'Making America Great Again' (MAGA) captures Trump's populism, giving voice to the role played by perceived threats to status and identity in the formation of foreign policy (Mounk and Kyle, 2018). This serves the purpose of capturing the political and rhetorical essence of Trump's campaign. MAGA populism draws on recent historical experience with the Tea Party movement, and deeper Jacksonian threads. The word *again* in MAGA provides a sense that something fundamental has been lost. What is it? Mead offers an answer: the federal government's role of ensuring the American "physical security and economic well-being" at home with as little interference as possible (Mead, 2017, 2). This includes protecting American sovereignty from international institutions which require states to cede a measure of control to international laws and norms. On this Jeff Colgan and Robert Keohane write that "The cumulative effect of such expansions of international authority is to excessively limit sovereignty and give people the sense that foreign forces are controlling their lives" (2017, 42). Jacksonians, wary and skeptical of international institutions, offer to return control and sovereignty to the people.

A common impression is that the motivation for many to vote for Trump was economic dislocation. Porter (2016) wrote that the areas where Trump did well were also areas still smarting from loss of income during the Great Recession. Nate Silver argues, however, that education rather than income explains the 2016 election outcome (Silver, 2016). He holds that educational achievement determined the difference in election outcomes between 2012 and 2016. Mutz contends otherwise, arguing that perceived loss of status, felt most intently by some white Christian men, was the prime driver of voting for Trump (Mutz, 2018). A distant echo of Mutz's post-election analysis is the pre-election polemicist, Michael Anton (writing under the pseudonym Publius Decius Mus), who wrote in September 2016: "This is the mark of a party [the GOP], a society, a country, a people, a civilization that wants to die. Trump, alone among candidates for high office in this or in the last seven (at least) cycles, has stood up to say: I want to live. I want my party to live. I want my country to live. I want my people to live" (Anton, 2016).

The above translates into a Jacksonian version of American exceptionalism, grounded in the "singular commitment to the equality and dignity of individual American citizens" (Mead, 2017, 2). The populist lens offered by Trump in his inaugural address is unmistakable.

"From this moment on, it's going to be America First. Every decision on trade, on taxes, on immigration, on foreign affairs, will be made to benefit American workers and American families. We must protect our borders from the ravages of other countries making our products, stealing our companies, and destroying our jobs. Protection will lead to great prosperity and strength" (White House, 2017). Taken together, this "great transformation" (Cha, 2017, 84) is spearheaded and led by the charismatic leadership of Donald Trump.

Conclusion

This chapter began by showing that Trump's 2016 presidential victory suggests he is capable of making tactically adroit decisions to achieve his ends, and engages often inflammatory, and unconventional, methods to do so. In contrast to the prevalent view among Trump's detractors that he is an idiot, he displays behavior that suggests he is an individual of considerable cunning. Trump's long-standing views on foreign policy were then outlined – issues that, as president, require him to take action at the international level and adjust US relations with friends, partners, and enemies. In short, isolationism was never on the cards. Rather, achieving US aims (through transactional deal-making) requires engaging others in a manner that tilts the balance of outcomes in US–other relations in Washington's favor. Existing deals that do not sufficiently benefit the US will be altered through re-negotiation and while the other side may get *something* it wants out of the bargain, it will not be as much as it received prior to the arrival of the Trump presidency. Trump clearly views himself as *the* decisive agent of change in the US – a 'genius' and master negotiator with skills acquired from his business career that are transferrable to the international realm; their application will redound in America's favor after a period of time when policies crafted by traditional elites did not. On this basis, Trump declared in his inauguration speech that as president "America will start winning again, winning like never before" (Trump, 2017).

A number of domestic factors buttressed Trump's 2016 victory, and support elements of his foreign policy as president. This includes public opinion conducive to aspects of a Trumpian foreign policy agenda even though on some issues it did not conform to his electoral positions – for example a majority of Americans viewed globalization, international trade, and alliances positively. Despite this, the primaries elevated candidates from both parties to power who called into question key elements of America's foreign policy (for Trump this extended across a range of issues; Clinton's major adjustment was to renounce her commitment to the TPP). Trump's ideas also overlapped with aspects of those put forward by the 'restraint constituency' – a set of intellectuals who asserted that US liberal hegemony had been extremely costly and unsustainable, proposing instead that the US adopt a more modest global posture based on realist principles with US allies increasing their security contributions.

The president is clearly comfortable working amongst, and even sowing, chaos to discombobulate his opponents. Furthermore, he is at home in using deception, misdirection, lying, and acting unpredictably to achieve his ends. Indeed, Trump's tactics of deception, which include little commitment to the truth, use of hyperbole, offensive tweets and statements, and constant self-contradictions may very well be beneficial in an age of mass information and political and media polarization. In other words, the contemporary information arena may be uniquely suited for an actor like Trump to take advantage. 'Winning' at any cost is the standard he adheres to. Nor does the president abide by a traditional political ideology; rather he has a ruthless dog-eat-dog view of the world where values have little role to play – he is 'value-free'. From this standpoint, for example, promoting democracy and opposing autocracy on principled and moral grounds are distractions and impede the US from seizing the initiative; it compels Washington to act in ways contrary to its interests.

To sum up, given the larger-than-life personality of the president and the ruthless determination (let alone the methods) he utilizes to pursue his ends, no consideration of his foreign policy can be divorced from the operating style and personal preferences outlined in this chapter. As we'll see in Chapters 3 and 4, they have infused his foreign policy tactics and strategy.

Notes

1 Peter Coleman writes that "One of the Trump team's most effective strategies for mobilizing support was to systematically study the emotional landscape of his potential supporters. Beginning in 2014, Trump assigned aides to listen to thousands of hours of talk radio and deliver reports on what most resonated with Republican voters. What they found was that immigration riled his base more than any other issue. This then became his signature campaign issue" (Coleman, 2019, 232).

2 Cha (2017, 84) writes: "Trump's rise is symptomatic of the ongoing great transformation of U.S. society during the worldwide economic stagnation. Angry populist forces have to a large extent altered the U.S. political landscape, thereby pushing the establishment to turn away from orthodox positions. In particular, existing liberal internationalist grand strategy is likely to be revised and gestured toward 'neo-isolationism'. We are

witnessing a historical watershed during which the direction of U.S. hegemony and the post-war liberal world order is beginning to change". Also see Aswad (2018).
3 The idea and theory of American exceptionalism has evolved over time, with a number of different discourses on the subject. On this see Cha (2015) and Song (2015).
4 As noted in the introduction, it is difficult to know when Trump is being honest about practically anything. A fact the president appears to welcome. Consider that Anthony Scaramucci, the former White House Communications Director, told *Washington Post* reporters that after he asked Trump if he was an "act" the president responded "I'm a total act and I don't understand why people don't get it" (Fink, 2020).

Bibliography

@realDonaldTrump, May 1, 2013.
@realDonaldTrump, May 30, 2014.
@realDonaldTrump, April 8, 2016.
@realDonaldTrump, October 2, 2016.
@realDonaldTrump, January 6, 2018.
@realDonaldTrump, June 4, 2018.
Adams, Scott. *Win Bigly: Persuasion in a World Where Facts Don't Matter.* New York: Portfolio, 2017.
Anton, Michael [writing under the pseudonym Publius Decius Mus]. The Flight 93 Election. *The Claremont Institute.* September 5, 2016. Retrieved from https://www.claremont.org/crb/basicpage/the-flight-93-election/.
Armbruster, Ben. Obama: 'America, It Is Time to Focus on Nation Building Here at Home'. June 23, 2011. *Thinkprogress.* Retrieved from https://thinkprogress.org/obama-america-it-is-time-to-focus-on-nation-building-here-at-home-c777e1c1b1f3/.
Aswad, Noor Ghazal. Exploring Charismatic Leadership: A Comparative Analysis of the Rhetoric of Hillary Clinton and Donald Trump in the 2016 Presidential Election. 2018. *Presidential Studies Quarterly*, 49(1): 56–74.
Berman, Russell. President Trump's 'Hard Power' Budget. March 16, 2016. *The Atlantic.* Retrieved from https://www.theatlantic.com/politics/archive/2017/03/president-trumps-hard-power-budget/519702/.
Bertoni, Steven. Exclusive Interview: How Jared Kushner Won Trump The White House, November 22, 2016, *Forbes.* Retrieved from https://www.forbes.com/sites/stevenbertoni/2016/11/22/exclusive-interview-how-jared-kushner-won-trump-the-white-house/#2cb307953af6.
Bonikowski, Bart. Ethno-Nationalist Populism and the Mobilization of Collective Resentment. 2017. *British Journal of Sociology*, 68(S1): 181–213.
Borger, Julian. Trump's Plan to Seize Iraq's Oil: "It's not stealing, we're reimbursing ourselves". September 21, 2016. *The Guardian.* Retrieved from https://www.theguardian.com/us-news/2016/sep/21/donald-trump-iraq-war-oil-strategy seizure-isis.

Borger, Julian. Rex Tillerson: 'America First' Means Divorcing our Policy from our Values. May 4, 2017. *The Guardian*. Retrieved from https://www.theguardian.com/us-news/2017/may/03/rex-tillerson-america-first-speech-trump-policy.

Borger, Julian. Trump Contradicts Aides and Says Troops in Syria 'Only for Oil'. November 13, 2019. *The Guardian*. Retrieved from https://www.theguardian.com/us-news/2019/nov/13/donald-trump-syria-oil-us-troops-isis-turkey.

Bosworth, Andrew. Thoughts for 2020. January 8, 2020. *Facebook*. Retrieved from https://www.facebook.com/boz/posts/10111288357877121.

Brands, Hal. *American Grand Strategy in the Age of Trump*. Washington, DC: Brookings Institution Press, 2018.

Brooks, Rosa. Donald Trump Has a Coherent, Realist Foreign Policy. April 12, 2016. *Foreign Policy*. Retrieved from https://foreignpolicy.com/2016/04/12/donald-trump-has-a-coherent-realist-foreign-policy/.

Brown, Michael E., Sean M. Lynn-Jones, and Steven E. Miller. *Debating the Democratic Peace*. Cambridge, MA: MIT Press, 1996.

Byers, Dylan. Donald Trump Has Earned $2 Billion in Free Media Coverage, Study Shows. March 15, 2016. *CNN*. Retrieved from https://money.cnn.com/2016/03/15/media/trump-free-media-coverage/.

Cassidy, John. Why Is Donald Trump in Michigan and Wisconsin. October 31, 2016. *The New Yorker*. Retrieved from https://www.newyorker.com/news/john-cassidy/why-is-donald-trump-in-michigan-and-wisconsin.

Cha, Taesuh. American Exceptionalism at the Crossroads: Three Responses. 2015. *Political Studies Review*, 13(3): 351–362.

Cha, Taesuh. The Return of Jacksonianism: The International Implications of the Trump Phenomenon. 2017. *Washington Quarterly*, 39(4): 83–97.

Cha, Taesuh, and Jungkun Seo. Trump by Nixon: Maverick Presidents in the Years of U.S. Relative Decline. 2018. *Korean Journal of Defense Analysis*, 30(1): 79–96.

Chappell, Bill. "I'm The Only One That Matters", Trump Says of State Dept. Job Vacancies. November 3, 2017. *NPR*. Retrieved from https://www.npr.org/sections/thetwo-way/2017/11/03/561797675/im-the-only-one-that-matters-trump-says-of-state-dept-job-vacancies.

Clarke, Michael, and Anthony Ricketts. Understanding the Return of the Jacksonian Tradition. 2017. *Orbis*, 61(1): 13–26.

Coleman, Peter T. Tentative Teachings on Conflict from Trump's Tumultuous Tenure in Office. January 29, 2019. *Negotiation Journal*, 35(1): 231–234.

Colgan, Jeff D., and Robert O. Keohane. The Liberal Order is Rigged: Fix It Now or Watch It Wither. May/June 2017. *Foreign Affairs*, 96(3): 36–44. Retrieved from https://www.foreignaffairs.com/articles/world/2017-04-17/liberal-order-rigged.

Contiguglia, Cat. Trump: EU Is One of United States' Biggest Foes. July 15, 2018. *Politico*. Retrieved from https://www.politico.eu/article/donald-trump-putin-russia-europe-one-of-united-states-biggest-foes/.

Coppins, McKay. The Heir. October 2019. *The Atlantic*. Retrieved from https://www.theatlantic.com/magazine/archive/2019/10/trump-dynasty/596674/.

Daalder, Ivo H., and James M. Lindsay. *The Empty Throne: America's Abdication of Global Leadership.* New York: Public Affairs, 2018.

Dueck, Colin. *Age of Iron: On Conservative Nationalism.* New York: Oxford University Press, 2019.

Eatwell, Roger. The Concept and Theory of Charismatic Leadership. 2006. *Totalitarian Movements and Political Religions,* 7(2): 141–156.

Edwards, Jason A. Make America Great Again: Donald Trump and Redefining the U.S. Role in the World. 2018. *Communication Quarterly,* 66(2): 176–195.

Factbase. Speech: Donald Trump in Rome, NY. April 12, 2016. *YouTube.* Retrieved from https://www.youtube.com/watch?time_continue=1545&v=6NsibpSxBUE&feature=emb_logo.

Fink, Jenni. Anthony Scaramucci Claims Trump Told Him He's a 'Total Act' in New Book. January 15, 2020. *Newsweek.* Retrieved from https://www.newsweek.com/anthony-scaramucci-claims-trump-told-him-hes-total-act-new-book-washington-post-reporters-1482420.

Fox News. Donald Trump Says America Has to Be "Less Predictable". November 3, 2015. *YouTube.* Retrieved from https://www.youtube.com/watch?v=mfrfrHLQWYk.

Freedom House. *Democracy in Crisis.* 2018. Retrieved from https://freedomhouse.org/report/freedom-world/freedom-world-2018.

Gajanan, Mahita. Read Donald Trump and Enrique Peña Nieto's Full Press Conference Statement. August 31, 2016. *CNN.* Retrieved from https://time.com/4475102/donald-trump-enrique-pena-nieto-transcript/.

Garcia, Feliks. Donald Trump Foreign Policy Speech: 5 Contradictions in the Presidential Hopeful's Plan. April 28, 2016. *The Independent.* Retrieved from https://www.independent.co.uk/news/world/americas/donald-trump-foreign-policy-speech-5-contradictions-in-the-presidential-hopefuls-plan-a7005711.html.

Georgantopoulos, Mary Ann. CNN's President Says It Was a Mistake to Air So Many Trump Rallies and "Let Them Run". October 14, 2016. *Buzzfeed.* Retrieved from https://www.buzzfeednews.com/article/maryanngeorgantopoulos/cnn-president-mistake-to-air-so-many-trump-rallies.

Gerges, Fawaz A. The Obama Approach to the Middle East: The End of America's Moment? 2013. *International Affairs,* 89(2): 299–323.

Gholz, Eugene, Daryl G. Press, and Harvey M. Sapolsky. Come Home, America: The Strategy of Restraint in the Face of Temptation. 1997. *International Security* 21(4): 5–48.

Gillin, Joshua. Bush says Trump was a Democrat Longer than a Republican 'In the Last Decade'. August 24, 2015. *Politifact.* Retrieved from https://www.politifact.com/factchecks/2015/aug/24/jeb-bush/bush-says-trump-was-democrat-longer-republican-las/.

Goldhill, Olivia. Rhetoric Scholars Pinpoint Why Trump's Inarticulate Speaking Style is so Persuasive. April 22, 2017. *Quartz.* Retrieved from https://qz.com/965004/rhetoric-scholars-pinpoint-why-trumps-inarticulate-speaking-style-is-so-persuasive/.

Guinote, Ana. How Power Affects People: Activating, Wanting, and Goal Seeking. 2017. *Annual Review of Psychology*, 68(1): 353–381.

Hartmann, Margaret. Trump Declines to Say He Supports Bannon, Declares, 'I'm My Own Strategist'. April 12, 2017. *New York Magazine*. Retrieved from http://nymag.com/intelligencer/2017/04/trump-downplays-bannon-role.html.

Heisbourg, François. The Emperor vs the Adults: Donald Trump and Wilhelm II. 2017. *Survival* 9(2): 7–12.

Hudson, John. Senators Slam NATO 'Free-Riders' in Closed-Door Meeting with Secretary General. April 6, 2016. *Foreign Policy*. Retrieved from https://foreignpolicy.com/2016/04/06/senators-slam-nato-free-riders-in-closed-door-meeting-with-secretary-general/.

Igielnik, Ruth, and Kim Parker. Majorities of U.S. Veterans, Public say the Wars in Iraq and Afghanistan were not Worth Fighting. July 10, 2019. *Pew Research*. Retrieved from https://www.pewresearch.org/fact-tank/2019/07/10/majorities-of-u-s-veterans-public-say-the-wars-in-iraq-and-afghanistan-were-not-worth-fighting/.

Kaczynski, Andrew. The Donald Trump Foreign Policy Doctrine, As Explained In His 2000 Book. September 28, 2015. *Buzzfeed*. Retrieved from https://www.buzzfeednews.com/article/andrewkaczynski/peace-through-hair.

Kessler, Glenn, Salvador Rizzo, and Meg Kelly. President Trump Made 16,241 False or Misleading Claims in His First Three Years. January 20, 2020. *The Washington Post*. https://www.washingtonpost.com/politics/2020/01/20/president-trump-made-16241-false-or-misleading-claims-his-first-three-years/.

Kirkland, Allegra. Political Pros See No Logic in Trump's All-Over-The-Map Campaign Schedule. October 28, 2016. *Talking Points Memo*. Retrieved from https://talkingpointsmemo.com/news/campaign-strategists-say-trump-packed-schedule-makes-no-sense.

Klein, Ezra. Donald Trump Will Never Be Able to Reinvent Himself as a Moderate. April 25, 2016. *Vox*. Retrieved from https://www.vox.com/2016/4/25/11498654/donald-trump-reinvent-moderate.

Kogan, Eugene B. Art of the Power Deal: The Four Negotiation Roles of Donald J. Trump. 2019. *Negotiation Journal*, 35(1): 65–83.

Laderman, Charlie, and Brendan Simms. *Donald Trump: The Making of a World View*. New York: I.B. Tauris, 2017.

Lake, Anthony. From Containment to Enlargement. September 21, 1993. Retrieved from www.disam.dsca.mil/pubs/Vol%2016_2/Lake.pdf.

Levinger, Mathew. Love, Fear, Anger: The Emotional Arc of Populist Rhetoric. 2017. *Narrative and Conflict*, 6(1): 1–21.

Lissner, Rebecca Friedman, and Mira Rapp-Hooper. The Day after Trump: American Strategy for a New International Order. 2018. *The Washington Quarterly*, 41(1): 7–25.

Lukes, Steven. The Big Picture: Trump's Charisma. October 25, 2017. *Public Books*. Retrieved from https://www.publicbooks.org/big-picture-trumps-charisma/.

McMaster, H. R., and Gary Cohn. America First Doesn't Mean America Alone. *Wall Street Journal.* May 30, 2017. Retrieved from https://www.wsj.com/articles/america-first-doesnt-mean-america-alone-1496187426.

Mead, Walter Russell. 2017. The Jacksonian Revolt: American Populism and the Liberal Order. March/April 2017. *Foreign Affairs*, 96(2): 2–8.

Mearsheimer, John J. *Great Delusion: Liberal Dreams and International Realities.* New Haven, CT: Yale University Press, 2018.

Mearsheimer, John, and Stephen Walt. The Case for Offshore Balancing: A Superior U.S. Grand Strategy. July/August 2016. *Foreign Affairs*, 95(4): 70–83.

Mounk, Yascha, and Jordan Kyle. What Populists Do to Democracies. December 26, 2018. *The Atlantic.* Retrieved from https://www.theatlantic.com/ideas/archive/2018/12/hard-data populism-bolsonaro-trump/578878/.

Mutz, Diana. Status Threat, Not Economic Hardship, Explains the 2016 Presidential Vote. 2018. *Proceedings of the National Academy of Sciences of the United States of America*, 115(19): E4330–E4339.

Netflix. Get Me Roger Stone. 2017. Documentary.

Netflix. Trump: An American Dream. 2018. Documentary.

Nunn, Gary. Winning Words: The Language that Got Donald Trump Elected. November 11, 2016. *The Guardian.* Available at https://www.theguardian.com/media/mind-your-language/2016/nov/11/winning-words-the-language-that-got-donald-trump-elected.

Patterson, Thomas. New Paper Examines Presidential Campaign Media Coverage Pre-primaries. June 24, 2016. *Harvard Kennedy School.* Retrieved from https://www.hks.harvard.edu/research-insights/policy-topics/politics/new-paper-examines-presidential-campaign-media-coverage.

PBS. How Photographer Platon Gets Up Close to Capture a Person's Truth. April 6, 2017. Retrieved from https://www.youtube.com/watch?v=xBcVIqCx3fY&feature=emb_logo.

Pew Research Center. Public Uncertain, Divided Over America's Place in the World. May 5, 2016. Retrieved from https://www.people-press.org/2016/05/05/public-uncertain-divided-over-americas-place-in-the-world/.

Plaskin, Glenn. The 1990 Playboy Interview with Donald Trump. March 1, 1990. *Playboy.* Retrieved from https://www.playboy.com/read/playboy-interview-donaldtrump-1990.

Pocalyko, Michael. The Businessman President. 2017. *Survival*, 59(1): 51–57.

Porter, Esuardo. Where Were Trump's Votes? Where the Jobs Weren't. December 13, 2016. *New York Times.* Retrieved from https://www.nytimes.com/2016/12/13/business/economy/jobs-economy-voters.html.

Posen, Barry. *Restraint: A New Foundation for U.S. Grand Strategy.* New York: Cornell University Press, 2014.

RealClearPolitics. General Election: Trump vs. Clinton. 2016. Retrieved from https://www.realclearpolitics.com/epolls/2016/president/us/general_election_trump_vs_clinton-5491.html.

Rovere, Crispin. Trump's Foreign Policy: America First, not America Only. November 17, 2016. *Lowy Institute.* Retrieved from https://www.lowyinstitute. org/the-interpreter/trumps-foreign-policy-america-first-not-america-only.

Savoy, Jacques. Trump's and Clinton's Style and Rhetoric during the 2016 Presidential Election. 2018. *Journal of Quantitative Linguistics* 25(2): 168–189.

Schuessler, John. Why Does Donald Trump Have So Much Trouble with the Truth? In (eds.) Jervis, Robert, et al. *Chaos in the Liberal Order: The Trump Presidency and International Politics in the Twenty-First Century.* New York: Columbia University Press, 2018.

Sclafani, Jennifer. *Talking Donald Trump: A Sociolinguistic Study of Style, Metadiscourse, and Political Identity.* Abingdon: Routledge, 2018.

Shell, G. Richard. Transactional Man: Teaching Negotiation Strategy in the Age of Trump. 2019. *Negotiation Journal,* 35(1): 31–45.

Shepard, Steven. Democratic Insiders: Clinton's Ground Game Will Sink Trump. November 4, 2016. *Politico.* Retrieved from https://www.politico.com/story/ 2016/11/democratic-insiders-hillarys-ground-game-will-sink-trump-230718.

Shirer, William L. *The Rise and Fall of the Third Reich: A History of Nazi Germany.* London: Pan Books, 1964.

Silver, Nate. Education, Not Income, Predicted Who Would Vote for Trump. November 22, 2016. *Fivethirtyeight.* Retrieved from https://fivethirtyeight. com/features/education-not-income-predicted-who-would-vote-for-trump/.

Silver, Nate. The Real Story of 2016. 2017. *Fivethirtyeight.* Retrieved from https://fivethirtyeight.com/tag/the-real-story-of-2016/.

Smith, Candace, and Liz Kreutz. Hillary Clinton's and Donald Trump's Campaigns by the Numbers. November 8, 2016. *ABC News.* Retrieved from https://abcnews.go.com/Politics/hillary-clinton-donald-trumps-campaigns-numbers/story?id=43356783.

Song, Seongjong. American Exceptionalism at a Crossroads. April 2015. *Korean Journal of International Studies,* 13(1): 239–262.

Swift, Art. Americans' Trust in Mass Media Sinks to New Low. September 14, 2016. *Gallup.* Retrieved from https://news.gallup.com/poll/195542/americans-trust-mass-media-sinks-new-low.aspx.

Taranto, James. Dilbert Explains Donald Trump. August 19, 2016, *Wall Street Journal.* Retrieved from https://www.wsj.com/articles/dilbert-explains-donald-trump-1471645144.

Tatum, Sophie. Trump Defends Putin: 'You Think Our Country's So Innocent?' February 6, 2017. *CNN.* Retrieved from https://edition.cnn.com/ 2017/02/04/politics/donald-trump-vladimir-putin/index.html.

Time. Here's Donald Trump's Presidential Announcement Speech. June 16, 2015. *Time.* Retrieved from https://time.com/3923128/donald-trump-announcement-speech/.

Trump, Donald (a). Trump on Foreign Policy. April 27, 2016. *National Interest.* Retrieved from https://nationalinterest.org/feature/trump-foreign-policy-15960.

Trump, Donald (b). Transcript of Donald Trump's Immigration Speech. September 1, 2016. *New York Times*. Retrieved from https://www.nytimes.com/2016/09/02/us/politics/transcript-trump-immigration-speech.html.

Trump, Donald. Inaugural Address. White House. 2017. Retrieved from https://www.whitehouse.gov/briefings-statements/the-inaugural-address/.

Trump, Donald, and Tony Schwartz. *Trump: The Art of the Deal*. New York: Ballantine Books, 2015 edition.

Vitali, Ali. Trump, Once Critical from Afar, Gives China a Pass in Trade War. November 9, 2017. *NBC*. Retrieved from https://www.nbcnews.com/news/world/trump-says-he-doesn-t-blame-china-taking-advantage-u-n819221.

Wall Street Journal. President Trump's Interview with the *Wall Street Journal*. November 26, 2018. Retrieved from https://www.wsj.com/articles/transcript-of-president-trumps-interview-with-the-wall-street-journal-1543272091.

Walt, Stephen M. *The Hell of Good Intentions: America's Foreign Policy Elite and the Decline of U.S. Primacy*. New York: Farrar, Straus and Giroux, 2018.

Weber, Max. *The Theory of Social and Economic Organization*. New York: Free Press, 1947.

Wells, Chris, Dhavan V. Shah, Jon C. Pevehouse, JungHwan Yang, Ayellet Pelled, Frederick Boehm, et al. How Trump Drove Coverage to the Nomination: Hybrid Media Campaigning. 2016. *Political Communication*, 33(4): 669–676.

Wertheim, Stephen. Trump against Exceptionalism: The Sources of Trumpian Conduct. In (eds.) Jervis, Robert, et al. *Chaos in the Liberal Order: The Trump Presidency and International Politics in the Twenty-First Century*. New York: Columbia University Press, 2018.

Wright, Thomas. Trump's 19th Century Foreign Policy. January 20, 2016. *Politico*. Retrieved from https://www.politico.com/magazine/story/2016/01/donald-trump-foreign-policy-213546.

3 The 'art of the deal'

The Trump administration's foreign policy tactics

Introduction

This chapter examines patterns of behavior behind the Trump administration's discordant tactics. It carries over the *individual level* of analysis from Chapter 1, showing how Trump's experience as a businessman influences two key tactics Trump has employed since his election in 2016. It contains three sections. The first establishes a frame of reference for understanding Trump's seemingly erratic approach to foreign policy. This includes recognition of President Trump as a *tactical opportunist* and consideration of his self-perception (some would say self-styled mythology) that stems from his pre-political career as a businessman. Section two considers two key methods. The first comprises the administration's 'art of the deal', with its approach to NATO, trade with China, Mexico and Canada, and negotiations over the North Korean nuclear program offered as examples. It also briefly considers whether negotiations have worked in each case and posits that Trump's threats in one negotiation are connected with decisions he makes on other international issues that generate additional leverage. The second tactic is the president's use of the 'rationality of irrationality', which draws upon post-war strategic theory but is also consistent with his personality. Furthermore, what should become evident to the reader is that Trump's behavior and rhetoric suit his negotiation style and are explicable as unpredictable maneuvers; there is a symbiosis between the two tactics. The third and concluding section makes the case that the evidence surveyed throughout the chapter confirms that President Trump employs a negotiation style that stem from pre-presidential business experience. It also considers whether these methods have achieved the objectives the administration has set itself and predicts it is unlikely Trump will deviate from these tactics for the remainder of his presidency.

Trump the tactical opportunist and negotiation artist

President Trump's approach to foreign policy is similar to that which he employs in the domestic arena. He constantly 'flip-flops' – reverses his position – on major issues depending on what he believes will benefit him in the moment. In this sense, he operates as a *tactical opportunist*. Amongst other issues, this has included changing his positions on abortion, torture, taxes on the wealthy, banning Muslims from entering the US, immigration, gun control regulations, his view of a number of politicians, climate change, torture, the wisdom of invading Iraq, whether it's advisable for Japan to acquire nuclear weapons, attacking Syria, joining the TPP, American commitment to Article V of NATO, and his views on China. As Chapter 1 explained, Trump has a great deal of conviction about himself and what serves his ends in the moment but everything else – individuals, policies, and principles – are expedient and can be rapidly replaced to get what he wants. The constant shuffling of senior administration personnel in the first months of his administration speaks to this (Tenpas, Kamarck, and Zeppos, 2018), as does his conduct throughout the 2016 election campaign (refer to Chapter 1).

President Trump considers himself to be a master negotiator and expert businessman. In his conceptualization contemporary US foreign policy can be a reflection and extension of his unique business acumen, with the approach to business and negotiations he adopted during his pre-presidential career applied to international negotiations. To Trump, what works domestically should work internationally. He made this clear in *The America We Deserve*, arguing that in the post-Cold War world:

> I believe that the day of the chess player is over. American foreign policy has to be put in the hands of a dealmaker ... A true dealmaker can keep many balls in the air, weigh the competing interests of other nations, and, above all, constantly put America's best interests first. The true dealmaker knows when to be tough and when to back off ... He knows when to bluff and he knows when to threaten, understanding that you threaten only when prepared to carry out the threat.
>
> (Trump and Shiflett, 2000, 112)

Trump believes he is indispensable to successful negotiations, revealing a preference for centralized leadership that informs his negotiation approach. "If you're going to make a deal of any significance," he once wrote, "you have to go to the top" (Trump and Schwartz, 2015, 127).

Trump links the success of his bargaining strategy to his unique instincts, likening himself to an "artist" with skills that allow him to make "big" and "complicated" deals: "deal-making is an ability you're born with. It's in the genes ... it's about instincts" (Ibid., 32).[1] Indeed, a "keen instinct for risk and opportunity" is a typical trait of the 'billionaire personality'; it is apparently key to their ability to seize opportunities others cannot (UBS/PwC, 2015).[2]

Trump is credited as co-authoring a number of business-advice books, including the *Art of the Deal*. First published in 1987, it became a *New York Times* bestseller, made Trump a household name in the US, and is the fifth highest selling business-advice book of all time (Qiu, 2015). It professes to contain the philosophy behind his success, declaring: "My style of deal-making is quite simple and straightforward ... I aim very high, and then I just keep pushing and pushing to get what I'm after. Sometimes I settle for less than I sought, but in most cases I still end up with what I want" (Trump and Schwartz, 2015, 45). While many negotiators initially aim high, scholars of negotiation theory such as Richard Shell note that Trump pursues "super aggressive expectations" based upon a "dream big" approach utilized throughout his business career (Shell, 2019, 40).[3] He puts forward "an outrageous opening offer" that anchors his opponents to his "end of the bargaining range" and may threaten to walk away unless his interlocutors shift closer to his position (Ibid., 42). Trump continues: "I play it very loose ... I prefer to come to work each day and just see what develops ... I just keep pushing and pushing and pushing to get what I'm after ... The best thing you can do is deal from strength, and *leverage is the biggest strength you have.* Leverage is having something the other guy wants. Or better yet, needs" (Trump and Schwartz, 2015, 112). To Trump: "how far a negotiator can push depends on his or her leverage" and to Shell "Transactional Man [Trump] is a doer, and a single-minded focus on leverage can compensate for many negotiation mistakes" (Shell, 2019, 42–43).

Identifying and amassing leverage (what the other side wants) requires empathy. Brian Rathbun criticized Trump for lacking this capacity, noting that "This awareness of others' interests is at the heart of realpolitik, and its absence [in Trump] is what drives realists most crazy" (Rathbun, 2018, 100). But Shell explains that for Trump his empathy exists not to care about another's emotions, but "to discover the weaknesses in an opponent's position, exploit them as fully as possible, and maximize leverage" (2019, 44). As such, Trump explained in 2009 that a key to a successful negotiation is "to be able to size up your opponent", and in 2006 he recommended: "Learn your adversary's strengths and weaknesses: Find out who your adversaries are, what resources they have, who is backing them, how much they want, why they want it, how much they will settle for, and how much they will pay or insist on receiving" (Kogan, 2019, 68).

By setting a super aggressive negotiation position and identifying relevant leverage, Trump then offers "a drastic structured choice to his opponents, leaving them the least manoeuvring space ... The structured choice approach is powerful because Trump essentially narrows down the other party's choice set to only two options: one with a clear incentive and the other with an unpredictable (potentially, devastating) threat" (Ibid., 70). For example, when discussing US relations with Russia on July 19, 2018, Trump said: "Getting along with President Putin ... is a positive, not a negative. Now ... if that doesn't work out, I'll be the worst enemy he's ever had ... I'll be his worst nightmare" (Ibid., 73). And when it came to Turkey's invasion of northern Syria in October 2019 he tweeted "As I have stated strongly before, and just to reiterate, if Turkey does anything that I, in my great and unmatched wisdom, consider to be off limits, I will totally destroy and obliterate the Economy of Turkey (I've done before!)" (@realDonaldTrump, October 8, 2019).[4]

Furthermore, the idea of aiming "very high" and "pushing and pushing" is consistent with the president's long-standing theme of "getting tough" and, in Trump's mind, the country's top leaders and negotiators are not in politics but reside in the cut-throat world of business (Laderman and Simms, 2017, 27, 29). As such, despite pledging to 'drain the swamp' during the 2016 election campaign, Trump stacked his Cabinet with executives, bankers, millionaires and billionaires, defending his choices by stating, "I want people that made a fortune because now they're negotiating with you ... It's no different than a great baseball player or a great golfer" (Cranley, 2019). Surrounding himself with tough negotiators is a practice from Trump's business days. On this, Shell writes: "Trump surrounded himself with skilled, ruthless Transactional Men who were as good as, or better than, he was at hard-ball negotiation" (2019, 33). This speaks to an important point: Trump, generally, does not lead negotiations, rather he acts as the team's chief strategist. Shell continues: "He was seldom the front-line negotiator. Rather, he was the chief strategist for a Transactional Man negotiation team" (Ibid., 34). Two of Trump's key employees (both lawyers) were Roy Cohn (who considered Trump his protégé),[5] described by Ken Auletta as "a legal executioner – the toughest, meanest, loyalist, vilest, and one of the most brilliant lawyers in America" and "the other a lesser-known but equally aggressive real estate attorney named George Ross" (Ibid., 34–35).

Describing how he worked with Ross, Trump wrote: "I like to work in broad strokes, deal with the big picture, but not the details. For the details, I rely almost entirely on George. He is able to put my vision into concrete terms, but he is also a natural at judging how any given negotiation needs to proceed; what the other side wants and needs; and how to get results" (quoted in Ibid., 37). On Cohn Trump stated: "Roy [Cohn] was brutal, but he was a very loyal guy. He brutalized for you" (Ibid., 36).

Trump's obsessive focus on winning and seeming absence of morality means that a "virtually unlimited set of tactics ethically [are] available to him" (Shell, 2019, 33). When Ross was asked, "Are lying, cheating, and deception permitted?" in Trump's playbook, Ross (Ibid., 33) replied, "Yes, anything goes ... virtually anything other than unambiguous fraud is acceptable before a deal is signed, and breaching contracts is fine if a cost-benefit calculation justifies it" (Ibid., 41). Unsurprisingly, existing deals or arrangements that he seeks to change in America's favor are judged to be unfair; rhetoric that we can imagine plays well to his domestic audience.

Throughout the 2015–2016 election campaign, Trump repeatedly argued that, unlike traditional presidents, he was uniquely qualified to identify opportunities and weaknesses in America's negotiating partners and competitors – his skills and unscrupulous methods offered the US advantages over other actors not proficient in their use and who play by the more conventional rules of political conduct. Shell suggests there may be a basis for this, explaining that "Very few [negotiation] classes provide in-depth training on how to defend against the kind of aggressive, emotionally manipulative moves that Trump, Cohn, and Ross specialized in" (2019, 43). Through his insights and methods, Trump would seize the initiative on a raft of issues. Moving swiftly and disrupting the status quo would be key. On this point, Michael Pocalyko explains that Trump, as a graduate from the Wharton School of the University of Pennsylvania, should be expected to "disrupt the status quo deliberately and enthusiastically, to move proactively, and to take advantage of all circumstances and forces of disruption – whether or not he has catalysed them. This is the context of the new US administration as an arc continuing the president's five decades in global business and his conduct of a sui generis 2016 presidential campaign" (Pocalyko, 2017, 52). And when it comes to foreign policy, Pocalyko believes "Trump will use future international disruptions to underscore core elements of his own policies – quickly, reactively and in real time" (Ibid., 53).

The next section explains how Trump's supposedly unique skills that allowed him to conduct 'complicated' negotiations and secure 'big' deals during his pre-presidential career have now been transferred into the foreign policy domain.

Foreign policy tactics of the Trump administration

Tactic 1: The 'art of the deal': Trump's negotiating strategy

From Trump's business practices and stated philosophy, his approach to foreign policy should reflect his personal preference for "hard bargaining" tactics. He and his aides will initially aim very high – sometimes setting outrageous opening positions – to anchor the bargaining range towards his end. These will be backed up with rhetorical threats to impose severe penalties or take actions his negotiating partners or target states (for example rogue regimes) will find undesirable or costly unless they are willing to compromise.

During the US election campaign Trump pledged, or threatened, that once in office he would consider implementing a number of controversial foreign policy positions. A non-exhaustive list of these included:

The US might allow the breakup of NATO
The US might leave the North American Free Trade Agreement (NAFTA)
The US might allow Japan/South Korea to acquire nuclear weapons
The US might withdraw its military from South Korea
The US would place tariffs on China (imposed)
The US would leave the TPP (completed)
The US would leave the Paris (climate) Agreement (in process).

A number of these were not completely unprecedented. For example the Bush administration did not ratify the Kyoto Protocol climate pact; American presidents have complained about NATO free-riding for decades; Jimmy Carter wanted to drawdown US military forces from South Korea; and the US has assisted some countries in acquiring nuclear arms or ignored their efforts to do so (like Britain, France, Israel, and Pakistan). But the positions Trump laid out came as a shock to the world, especially given the manner and language Trump used to issue them, and the sheer number of them. The fact he was a political outsider and was reportedly largely uninformed about international affairs no doubt reinforced concerns.[6]

Yet, it was hard to take the slate of positions seriously for the reason that executing some, let alone all of them, would incur significant material costs, damage US soft power, and undermine US credibility with partners and allies. At worst, it threatened to lead to a decisive decline in US global influence and collapse the extended US alliance structure, developments that would play into the hands of America's competitors and adversaries. An explicable rationale exists for such an assortment of positions when interpreted as very high opening bids to anchor negotiations. Furthermore, launching a collective salvo of seemingly radical positions makes greater sense when considering them as interconnected with one another: a complicated set of negotiations or balls in the air. There is precedent here from Trump's business career, with Trump biographers Michael Kranish and Marc Fisher explaining that to secure his breakthrough development in the 1970s in the construction of the Grand Hyatt Hotel in Manhattan, "Trump played the city, the sellers, and the hotel chain off one another, using one to leverage a deal with the other" (Shell, 2019, 36).

Returning to the aforementioned set of issues, in isolation withdrawing from the TPP knocked a key pillar out of the Obama administration's Asia–Pacific strategy to offer states an economic alternative to the increasing pull of China (Tun-Jen and Chow, 2014; Chow, 2016; Dai, 2015); US withdrawal from the Paris Agreement on climate change resulted in widespread international criticism, and made the US a global outlier (the treaty has 195 signatories). Why pursue these actions? Within an interconnected negotiating framework, these decisions can generate leverage for use on other foreign policy issues because they show that the administration *might actually* go through with some of its seemingly 'extreme' threats – including damaging its own interests and influence in the process. This is what South Korean legislator Won Yoo Chul called the "Trump risk" – the fear the president will one day suddenly tweet he is withdrawing US troops from the Korean Peninsula (Denyer and Kim, 2019). These concerns are not just a product of Trump's insistence that Seoul pay five times the existing amount to station US forces but, according to opposition politician Baek Seung-joo, stem from US behavior elsewhere, such as in Syria where Trump announced a sudden withdrawal of troops that were providing support to the Kurds in northern Syria (Ibid.; Breuninger, 2019).

Had the president not gone through with withdrawal from TPP then when renegotiating NAFTA with Mexico and Canada, it would be unlikely these states would believe the US would withdraw from the negotiations. By walking away from TPP, Mexico and Canada had to take his threats to withdraw from their trade grouping seriously, and thus it increased the prospects they would renegotiate the deal. They will suffer some costs by renegotiating NAFTA, but this outcome is preferable to the greater costs they would incur if the Trump administration were to withdraw completely, a move not outside the realm of possibility given his self-damaging withdrawals from other agreements. Finally, Trump's penchant to shift positions rapidly and unpredictable behavior (the second tactic discussed in this chapter) add additional credibility to his threats. Having outlined Trump's preferred approach to negotiations, the chapter now considers the 'art of the deal' in practice.

The 'art of the deal': Trade with China

Since 2011, Donald Trump has taken aim at trade with China, tweeting: "America's trade deficit with China is one of our greatest national security threats. Time for Fair Trade. We must produce our own products" (@realDonaldTrump, November 29, 2011). These views would remain unchanged, as throughout the 2015–2016 presidential election campaign Trump continued to target China's trade practices and framed himself as the only one who could effectively deal with Beijing. On July 21, 2015, he stated "I beat the people from China. I win against China. You can win against China if you're smart. But our people don't have a clue ... They're ripping us left and right" (Stracqualursi, 2017). He followed this in November 2015 saying "But when you see China, these are fierce people in terms of negotiation. They want to take your throat out, they want to cut you apart. These are tough people. I've dealt with them all my life" (Ibid.). He also recounted during a 2016 campaign rally, "I love China" and that he made lots of money doing business with the country (Ibid.). In Trump's understanding his knowledge of China and his 'tough' negotiating philosophy matches China's own 'tough' approach.

Upon entering office Trump signaled his intentions vis-à-vis China by picking 'tough' negotiators. This included Robert Lighthizer as US Trade Representative, a veteran lawyer who has represented steel companies in anti-dumping suits against China, and also considered a long-time China hawk (Donnan, 2018), and Peter Navarro as the director of the newly created National Trade Council. Navarro has written two books that strongly criticize China. The first, *The Coming China Wars: Where They Will Be Fought and How They Can Be Won,* describes China's government as corrupt, totalitarian, and bent on creating an empire (Navarro, 2007) and the second, *Death By China: Confronting the Dragon – A Global Call to Action*, contends China has adopted ruthless illegal economic measures that unfairly exploit America's economy (Navarro and Autry, 2011).

To establish an initial negotiating stance, during a major speech in June 2016 Trump declared that "China's entrance into the World Trade Organization has enabled the greatest jobs theft in history" (Politico, 2016). He made a number of explicit threats, stating that he was "going to instruct the U.S. Trade Representative to bring trade cases against China, both in this country and at the WTO" and "China's unfair subsidy behavior is prohibited by the terms of its entrance to the WTO, and I intend to enforce those rules" (Ibid.). He continued: "If China does not stop its illegal activities ... I will use every lawful presidential power to remedy trade disputes, including the application of tariffs consistent with Section 201 and 301 of the Trade Act of 1974 and Section 232 of the Trade Expansion Act of 1962" (Ibid.).

Trump's specific demands of China were considerable. They included (amongst others) that Beijing make structural reforms to their economy (including reducing state subsidization of key industries and corporations), reduce forced technology transfers from US firms operating in China, and give US businesses greater access to China's agriculture, energy, and financial markets. China did not give in as a trade war between the US and China ensued on July 6, 2018, when the US implemented a 25% tariff on 818 imported Chinese products (valued at $34bn) (Wong and Koty, 2019). From that point on, economic relations were characterized by periods of tit-for-tat tariffs (as of March 10, 2020, total US tariffs applied exclusively to Chinese goods are US$550bn, and total Chinese tariffs applied exclusively to US goods are US$185bn), followed by periods of truce and negotiation (Ibid.).

Trump has also attempted linkage – to connect other issues to US–China trade relations in order to up-the-ante and compel China to adjust its positions. For example, in September 2017, in the context of what was then an escalating spiral of tension between the US and North Korea, Trump tweeted: "The United States is considering, in addition to other options, stopping all trade with *any country* doing business with North Korea" (@realDonaldTrump, September 3, 2017). This would include China. Other issues, such as the decision in April 2018 by the US Department of Commerce to ban US companies from providing exports to ZTE (ZTE receives 25–30% of its components from US companies), a major Chinese telecommunications company, were also part of US efforts to enhance leverage in the trade dispute (Reuters, 2018). Yet, in an indication of Trump's transactional approach to foreign policy, he also signaled understanding of China's desire to protect its national interests, suggesting he expected compromise would, at some point, be possible (Politico, 2016). This is combined, in typical Trumpian fashion, with threats. For example, after the US applied the first set of tariffs against China in February 2018, the president followed this by signaling the US was in these negotiations for the long haul through a tweet on March 2, 2018, that said "trade wars are good, and easy to win" (@realDonaldTrump, March 2, 2018).

On January 15, 2020, a year and a half into the trade war, Trump signed a Phase I agreement alongside Chinese Premier Lie He at the White House. The deal includes clauses to strengthen intellectual property protections; a pledge by China to not force US companies to transfer technology to operate in China; an agreement to loosen China's barriers to food and agriculture as well as open China's financial services sector to US competitors; to loosen China's barriers to food and agriculture imports; to open China's financial services sector to US competitors; a pledge by both not to devalue their currencies, and establishment of a framework for officials to meet to discuss alleged violations. China also promised to purchase more US goods to the value of $200bn over the next two years (US Trade Representative, 2020). To secure the deal, the Trump administration agreed to not impose tariffs on an additional $160bn of Chinese goods, to reduce tariffs on another $112bn's worth and while 25% tariffs remain on $370bn in Chinese imports (Horsley, 2020), the administration can claim it has forged a new framework for US–China trade negotiations going forward.

The president claimed the deal marked "a sea change in international trade" he admitted it's "not everything ... There will be a 'Phase 2'" (Ibid.). This speaks to the fact that much of what is in the deal lacks teeth on the enforcement side and did not require China to change any law or regulation. Additionally, what will be central to securing a Phase II deal – getting the PRC to alter its state-centric model of capitalism and subsidization of key industries and corporations – will prove extremely difficult in follow-on negotiations.

The 'art of the deal': Trade with Mexico and Canada

From the beginning of his primary election campaign in 2015, Trump expressed dissatisfaction with NAFTA and Mexico's economic practices, stating "When do we beat Mexico at the border? ... they're killing us economically" (Time, 2015). In rhetoric he tied this to immigration, his signature campaign issue, stating "They're [Mexico] sending people that have lots of problems ... They're bringing drugs. They're bringing crime. They're rapists". To tackle these issues, he said "I will build a great, great wall on our southern border. And I will have Mexico pay for that wall" (Time, 2015). Trump claimed he was uniquely qualified to do this, citing his history of building real estate and interest in rebuilding America's infrastructure. Thus, his claim that "nobody builds walls better than me, believe me, and I'll build them very inexpensively" could credibly (if simplistically) be linked to his supposed business acumen (Ibid.).[7]

To position the US for future negotiations, Trump's campaign issued a hard-line position paper in August 2015 that declared "Mexico must pay for the wall and, until they do, the United States will, among other things: impound all remittance payments derived from illegal wages" (Farley, 2018). It also said it would increase fees on all temporary visas issued to Mexican CEOs and diplomats (and, if necessary, cancel them), increase fees on all NAFTA worker visas from Mexico and at ports of entry to the US from Mexico. It also pledged to consider placing tariffs on Mexico and cutting foreign aid (Ibid.). Trump followed this in September 2015 when, in an interview with 60 Minutes, he declared NAFTA had been "a disaster" and that as president the US would "either renegotiate it or we will break it" (60 Minutes, 2015).

Once in office, Trump issued a series of tweets prior to and during NAFTA negotiations with Mexico, linking the survival of a free trade agreement to his migration agenda and campaign pledge to build a wall. For example, in April 2018 he tweeted: "Mexico is doing very little, if not NOTHING, at stopping people from flowing into Mexico through their Southern Border, and then into the U.S ... They must stop the big drug and people flows, or I will stop their cash cow, NAFTA. NEED WALL!" (@realDonaldTrump, April 2, 2018). At other times he asked if NAFTA was "the worst economic deal in U.S. history?" (@realDonaldTrump, May 18, 2016) and said "I will renegotiate NAFTA. If I can't make a great deal, we're going to tear it up" (@realDonaldTrump, October 19, 2016). The Trump administration also indicated, and perhaps used as a negotiating device, the fact that it would reduce the eligible professions and number of visa renewals granted to Mexicans during the course of NAFTA renegotiations. In April 2018, Trump tweeted: "Mexico ... must stop people from going through Mexico and into the U.S. We may make this a condition of the new NAFTA Agreement" (Chiacu and Esposito, 2018). NAFTA renegotiations began on August 16, 2017.

Supplanting NAFTA, the US–Mexico–Canada agreement (USMCA) received bipartisan support[8] and was approved by the US Congress on January 16, 2020. The deal broadly mirrors many of NAFTA's provisions, and the aggregate benefit is expected to be moderate with the US International Trade Commission stating although the deal will have "a positive impact on U.S. trade, both with USMCA partners and with the rest of the world", it will create just 176,000 more US jobs over six years and increase Gross Domestic Product (GDP) by only 0.35% (United States International Trade Commission, 2019). Despite this, Trump claimed the USMCA was a great victory by providing increased dairy-market access for the US, a new sunset clause, and tougher auto rules (Bryan and Zeballos-Roig, 2019).

The 'art of the deal': NATO[9]

While a number of US presidents have expressed frustration over NATO's European members' inability or unwillingness to dedicate 2% of GDP to military spending (a figure set at the NATO summit in Wales in 2014), their protestations have been largely toothless. Trump sought to change this equation by establishing an extreme anchoring position, suggesting during the 2016 presidential race that he might accept the breakup of NATO (Parker, 2016). His tune did not change once he entered office. Just days after his inauguration he labeled the alliance "obsolete" since US allies were not contributing their fair share for their defense (Kaufman, 2017, 252) and not doing enough to fight terrorism (Ibid.; Benitez, 2019). Providing the rationale behind his assertive approach to strengthening the NATO alliance, in December 2017 he said "This is a major departure from the past, but a fair and necessary one—necessary for our country, necessary for our taxpayer, necessary for our own thought process" (White House, 2017b).

Trump's threats and pressure had the intended effect as it re-portedly caused "astonishment and agitation" across the alliance (Masters and Hunt, 2017). Trump kept the pressure on throughout 2017 and 2018. In May 25, 2017, during a major address to the leaders of NATO's member states in Belgium, Trump notably did not re-affirm US commitment to NATO's Article 5 on collective defense, declaring: "NATO members must finally contribute their fair share and meet their financial obligations, for 23 of the 28 member nations are still not paying what they should be paying and what they're supposed to be paying for their defense" (White House, 2017a). In December 2018 he tweeted: "The idea of a European Military didn't work out too well in W.W. I or 2. But the U.S. was there for you, and always will be. All we ask is that you pay your fair share of NATO. Germany is paying 1% while the U.S. pays 4.3% of a much larger GDP – to protect Europe. Fairness!" (@realDonaldTrump, December 9, 2018). Despite saying the US would "always" be there for its European NATO allies, in his typical fashion the president, in private, reportedly told senior administration officials throughout 2018 that he wanted to withdraw from the alliance (Barnes and Cooper, 2019). The (intentional or unintentional) leaking of such information no doubt kept allies off-guard. At other times he said that the "U.S. subsidizes [NATO] greatly!" (@realDonaldTrump, November 9, 2018) and "All NATO Nations must meet their 2% commitment, and that must ultimately go to 4%" (@realDonaldTrump, July 12, 2018). Trump's rhetorical embrace of authoritarian leaders (discussed in Chapter 4) also places pressure on America's European allies to show their commitment to NATO and America's security interests, as it suggests the US has alternative security allies (some which threaten European security) should they not pull their weight.

Trump's efforts to get America's NATO allies to contribute more to the alliance have produced mixed results. For context, all NATO members agreed in 2014 to progressively move towards spending 2% of GDP on defense by 2024. Since that time some members have accelerated towards this target, while others have made little headway. Trump's pressure appeared to work on the UK, which has kept its contribution at 2% despite budget projections in 2015–2016 showing it would slip to 1.8–1.9% (Raynova and Kearns, 2015). Germany will only spend 1.5% of GDP on defense by 2024, but made a positive move when it announced in November 2019 to move to 2% by 2031 (Emmott, 2019).

There are multiple factors at play here, with Trump's role just one of them. On this Simona Soare notes "The increase in defence spending in some European states is in no small measure due to President Trump's aggressive insistence and his transactional approach to the transatlantic partnership. However, it is not the only decisive factor. Indeed, two other strategic factors should not be discounted: the Russian threat and Europe's own realisation that it needs to be more responsible for its own defence and think more strategically about the competitiveness of its defence industry".[10] Meanwhile, Germany's Defense Minister Annegret Kramp-Karrenbauer added in November 2019 that Berlin is not doing this because "others are calling for it but because it is in the interest of our own security" (Emmott, 2019). Additionally, as Chapter 4 notes, this uptick may have occurred without the advent of the Trump administration as some European states had, prior to Trump, called for Europe to move towards greater strategic autonomy, strengthen the European defense industry and gain more leverage in NATO. Turning to notable failures we see that Europe's third and largest economies, France and Italy, have also both stubbornly resisted US pressure. The former's defense contribution as a share of GDP has declined since 2013, when it was 1.86%, to 1.22% in 2019. Meanwhile Italy's contribution decreased over the same period from 1.27% to 1.22% in 2019 (NATO, 2019).

The Trump administration did score a victory when a new scheme for allied contribution to the $2.5 billion NATO common budget (that funds NATO's headquarters, joint security investments, and some combined military operations) (Browne, 2019) was announced in November 2019. Although until this point contributions to the budget were intended to be proportionally related to the size of respective members' GDP, the US had taken on the burden of contributions for newer NATO allies, effectively contributing more than its fair share. The changes mean Washington's contribution will drop from 22% to 16%, with Germany raising its 14.8% contribution to 16% (Browne, 2019). The remainder of the shortfall will be made up by increased contributions from other NATO members (Browne, 2019).

Some prominent officials have supported Trump's approach. In January 2019, during a meeting with President Trump in Washington, NATO Secretary General Jens Stoltenburg stated "We agreed to do more to step up – and now we see the results. By the end of next year, NATO allies will add $100 billion extra toward defense … So we see some real money and some real results. And we see that the clear message from President Donald Trump is having an impact" (Cummings, 2019). Given a number of NATO states, especially central and eastern European ones, had already committed to increasing their defense budgets it is not clear whether Stoltenburg's quotes reflect genuine conviction or were just for show to placate Trump.

The 'art of the deal': North Korea

Virtually all of Trump's negotiation tactics have been on display during the US–North Korea nuclear negotiations. During a March trip to East Asia in 2017, then-Secretary of State Rex Tillerson declared an end to the policy of the Obama-era "strategic patience" as the administration turned to a policy of maximum pressure (McCurry, 2017). This included a new round of sanctions, deploying increased military assets to the region, and making overt appeals to China to try to use its influence to restrain the Democratic People's Republic of Korea's (DPRK) escalating missile and nuclear tests (Campbell, 2017). This pressure campaign was coupled with statements that suggested Trump sought negotiations, stating on May 1, 2017, that he would be "honored" to meet the North Korean leader, "if it's under … the right circumstances" (Borger, 2017). A structured choice was being prepared, but first verbal threats continued and tensions mounted. They seemed to reach a head when, in a speech to the UN in September 2017, President Trump vowed to "totally destroy North Korea" if it threatened the US, and he declared that "Rocket Man [Kim Jong-un] is on a suicide mission" (Buncombe, 2017). This was preceded in August by Trump's now infamous statement that North Korea should stop threatening the US or it could be "met with fire and fury and frankly power, the likes of which this world has never seen before" (Pramuk, 2017).

While Trump had suggested he could meet North Korea's leader under the right circumstances, it was still a surprise (including even to the South Korean officials that brought it up with him) when, in March 2018, Trump agreed to meet with Kim Jong-un. Yet this decision was in line with Trump's declaration in *The Art of the Deal* that transactions of significance require leaders "to go to the top" (Trump and Schwartz, 2015, 127), and in doing so he could size Kim up by identifying his weaknesses, strengths, and vulnerabilities. As far back as 1999 Trump had said the US needed to establish a personal understanding of North Korea's motives (Kogan, 2019, 75). Indeed, when announcing his decision to meet Kim he stated: "I think I'll know pretty quickly whether or not … something positive will happen. And if I think it won't happen, I'm not going to waste my time" (Ibid., 76). And when asked how he would 'read' North Korean dictator Kim Jong-un swiftly in their first meeting in June 2018, he said: "My touch, my feel, that's what I do" (Borger and Perkins, 2018). In a sign of seemingly good faith, Kim announced on April 21, 2018, that he was stopping nuclear and intercontinental ballistic missile tests (BBC, 2018).

At the opening of the summit in Singapore on June 12, 2018, a video made by the US National Security Council provided a structured choice for the North Korean dictator. It started by showing a rich prosperous North Korea before switching to show a scene of a nuclear explosion, while a narrator asked whether Kim would choose "To show vision and leadership? Or not?" It continued: "There can only be two results … one of moving back, or one of moving forward … It comes down to a choice … A great life, or isolation? Which path will he [Kim] choose?" (Kogan, 2019, 76–77).

Have negotiations borne fruit? Although the first summit concluded with a joint statement that called for new relations, a commitment by President Trump to provide security guarantees for North Korea; North Korea 'reaffirming' to complete denuclearization of the Korean Peninsula (through mutual confidence building); recovery of soldiers' remains from the Korean War, and a call for follow-up negotiations

(White House, 2018), North Korea did not commit to Complete Verifiable and Irreversible Dismantlement (CVID) (Westcott, 2018). Nor were any concrete technical details put forward for implementing the agreements. On the other hand, given the history between the DPRK and US, and North Korea's understandable concern that disarming could leave them vulnerable to future US regime change efforts (North Korea cited US regime change efforts against Libya and Iraq as reasons why they needed a nuclear deterrent) (Asia Times, 2016), an agreement to rapidly disarm was never likely. Instead a long-term, painstaking, and incremental process was always the more likely course of action, with tit-for-tat confidence-building efforts proving central to any diplomatic process.

Unsurprisingly, relations have been inconsistent. For example. Secretary Pompeo's August 2018 trip to Pyongyang was called off and then a Trump–Kim summit in Hanoi between Trump and Kim in February 2019 was cut short (Masterson, 2020). This was followed by a brief symbolic meeting on June 30, 2019, when Trump became the first sitting US president to stand on North Korean soil when he entered the Korean Demilitarized Zone (Arms Control Association, 2019).

But restraint was shown for much of 2019, as the Republic of Korea (ROK) and US decided in March 2019 to terminate their annual Key Resolve and Foal Eagle joint military drills, and in the same month the International Atomic Energy Agency (IAEA) announced that the DPRK had not operated its Yongbyon 5MW(e) reactor capable of producing weapons-grade plutonium since early December 2018 (Ibid.). Although the DPRK continued to launch short-range missiles throughout 2019, it did not launch any long-range missiles that are of concern to the US (given they could conceivably strike the US mainland or its Pacific territories). And while an escalatory phase could be imminent given Kim announced on January 1, 2020, that he was ending his nation's self-imposed moratorium on nuclear and international ballistic missile testing (Johnson, 2020), no test has occurred as of June 19, 2020.

In short, the evidence is mixed. Trump's tactics got the two leaders to the negotiating table. The relationship they established would appear to have gone some way to preventing another intense round of escalation between them, and the unpredictability of Trump (discussed more in the next section) and sensationalist presentation of structured choices could have convinced Pyongyang that de-escalation is in their interest. At best, it created a basis to move in the long term towards denuclearization and eventual

Korean reunification. At worst, its negotiations from the outset were a ruse by North Korea to bide time, try to break out of its international isolation, and continue to advance its nuclear and ballistic missile programs (primarily in the laboratory).

Tactic 2: The 'rationality of irrationality'

A lens for understanding Trump's unpredictable behavior and rhetorical outbursts lies in post-war writing on American strategic theory. In the post-war era, strategists grappled with how to make nuclear deterrent threats credible given they were predicated on being able to convince Soviet leaders that should they attack the US, its allies, or threaten vital American interests, the US would respond with a devastating retaliatory nuclear strike that would, in all likelihood, lead to the destruction of civilization (Schelling, 1966). Part of this involved coming up with elaborate ways to communicate this threat credibly, with Thomas Schelling positing that strategic actors could consciously choose to act in an irrational manner for rational purposes (Schelling, 1981). To Schelling, deterrence (and strategic interaction and competition more broadly) was akin to a bargaining situation between adversaries. In this situation, an actor (A) could behave in a manner the other side (B) perceives to be 'irrational'. In doing so, B will become uncertain about A's seemingly 'unpredictable' and dangerous behavior, which may lead them to back down during crucial strategic confrontations or in other situations. As such, A's irrational behavior can be viewed as rational given the expected payoff. Opponents may be less likely in general to take action at your expense over concerns that they simply do not know how you will respond.

The Iranians have used a version of this tactic (Fathi, 2005), the Soviet Union under Premier Nikita Khruschev practiced it (Khruscheva, 2017) and North Korea has been using it for decades (Cho, 2014). Even US presidents, such as Richard Nixon, spoke of a "Madman Theory" (Naftalo, 2017), telling his White House Chief of Staff H.R. Haldeman that:

> I call it the Madman Theory, Bob. I want the North Vietnamese to believe I've reached the point where I might do anything to stop the war. We'll just slip the word to them that, 'for God's sake, you know Nixon is obsessed about Communism. We can't restrain him when he's angry – and he has his hand on the nuclear button' – and Ho Chi Minh himself will be in Paris in two days begging for peace.
> (quoted in Sagan and Suri, 2003, 156)

Additionally, to try secure Soviet cooperation in assisting the US to wind down the war in Vietnam, Nixon's National Security Advisor Henry Kissinger wrote: "We must worry the Soviets about the possibility that we might lose our patience and may get out of control", and Nixon also said "I just want to keep them off balance. Keep them questioning what I will do" (Sechser and Fuhrmann, 2017, 5–6).

Despite the precedent Nixon set, what is unprecedented is an American president so consistently using this approach and directing it towards both allies and adversaries. It makes the US appear unreliable and a disruptive actor seeking to complicate international relations globally. In fact, this is a core and consistent pillar of the Trump administration's foreign policy. In a statement recorded by Jeffrey Goldberg, a senior Trump administration national-security official stated that part of the rationale underlying the "Trump Doctrine" is the belief that "Permanent destabilization creates American advantage" (Goldberg, 2018). Goldberg continues,

> The official who described this to me said Trump believes that keeping allies and adversaries alike perpetually off-balance necessarily benefits the United States, which is still the most powerful country on Earth. When I noted that America's adversaries seem far less destabilized by Trump than do America's allies, this official argued for strategic patience. 'They'll see over time that it doesn't pay to argue with us.'
>
> (Goldberg, 2018)

In an interview in January 2003 Trump critiqued the Bush administration's open telegraphing of plans to invade Iraq, "When I watch Dan Rather explaining how we are going to be attacking, where we're going to attack, what routes we're taking, what kind of planes we're using, how to stop them, how to stop us, it is a little bit disconcerting ... tell the enemy how we're going about it, we have just found out this and that. It is ridiculous" (Laderman and Simms, 2017, 64–65). In September 2013, he criticized Obama for backing down from his 'red line' in Syria, again reiterating the value of surprise rather than telegraphing US's military intentions in advance (Ibid., 89). And then in the run-up to the 2016 election he declared he would remain unpredictable to keep others off-guard, declaring in an interview with Fox News host Sean Hannity in November 2015 that: "I want to be much less – this country has to be less predictable" (Fox News, 2015). This position was reiterated during his first major foreign policy address as the Republican presidential candidate in April 2016: "We are totally predictable. We tell everything.

We're sending troops? We tell them. We're sending something else? We have a news conference. We have to be unpredictable, and we have to be unpredictable starting now" (Garcia, 2016). This principle even led him to refuse to rule out using nuclear weapons, stating "You don't want to say 'take everything off the table' because you're a bad negotiator if you say that … nuclear should be off the table, but would there be a time when it could be used? Possibly … I would never take any of my cards off the table" (Kogan, 2019, 70).

The 'rationality of irrationality' in practice

Trump's approach to numerous foreign policy issues suggests he acts irrationally to obtain leverage, and this is perhaps nowhere better displayed than in his interactions with North Korea and Iran. As noted, North Korea and Iran have at times used the very same tactics. Evidence suggests Trump also used it against Kim in the lead-up to the historic summit between the two leaders in June 2018 (even though this behavior conforms to Trump's negotiation tactics, examined above, through the lens adopted here they are also explicable as unpredictable maneuvers). Consider, in the year prior to this, and against the backdrop of North Korea expanding its nuclear long-range ballistic missile tests, both leaders threatened one another aggressively. This seemed to reach its apex in September 2017, when Trump issued the aforementioned statement that the US could face a situation where it would "have no choice but to totally destroy North Korea", and that "Rocket Man [Kim Jong-un] is on a suicide mission for himself and for his regime" (Nakamura and Gearan, 2017). Despite this, within seven months of Trump's statements at the UN, he stunned the world by accepting an invitation to meet Kim Jong-un at a summit in June 2018 (Baker, 2018). The unpredictable behavior continued when, in mid-May, North Korea threatened to cancel the summit in response to ongoing US–South Korea military exercises (Borger and McCurry, 2018). This announcement was seemingly irrational because the summit had been agreed to in the knowledge that these war games would continue in the lead-up. So why would North Korea do this? In all likelihood it was to continue to project an image of impulsiveness. In any event, Pyongyang did not go ahead and cancel the summit. Trump, for his part, responded a week later with a letter that (at the time) canceled the summit (Borger and Haas, 2018). This also seemed crazy and capricious but like North Korea's bluff, is consistent with Trump's stated desire to be unpredictable and, within a bargaining framework where being fickle is viewed as providing each side with leverage, the behavior of both suggests they were seeking leverage over the other through erratic behavior. Even South Korea has experienced Trump's volatility. For example, after Robert Lighthizer told Trump he would instruct the South Koreans that they had only 30 days to grant concessions to the US (to pay more to host US troops), Trump said "No, no, no ... That's not how you negotiate. You don't tell them they've got 30 days. You tell them, 'This guy's so crazy he could pull out any minute'". Trump continued, "That's what you tell them: Any minute ... And by the way, I might. You guys all need to know I might. You don't tell them 30 days. If they take 30 days they'll stretch this out" (Swan, 2017).

Trump has acted unpredictably towards Iran. Recent developments attest to this. In June 2019 evidence emerged that Tehran, likely in response to the Trump administration's 'maximum pressure' policy (which included withdrawal from the Joint Comprehensive Plan of Action, increasing sanctions, and strengthening the anti-Iran coalition in the region), asserted its power against US interests through an uptick in proxy attacks against US forces in the region and mining vessels transiting the Strait of Hormuz (Borger and Wintour, 2019a). This campaign culminated in Iran shooting down a US drone on June 20, 2019 (Turak, 2019). The administration – and Trump's response – was predictably unpredictable. Firstly, on the day the drone was shot down the president stated "I find it hard to believe it was intentional, if you want to know the truth ... I think that it could have been somebody who was loose and stupid that did it" (Borger and Wintour, 2019b). Yet, that very night, apparently a decision was made to conduct a limited military strike against Iranian radar and missile sites. At the last minute, despite US forces being "cocked and loaded", Trump called off the strike (Borger and Wintour, 2019c). This occurred, he said, because he was informed it would kill 150 people, which would be disproportionate to Iran's shooting down an unmanned US drone. It was also odd that the president reportedly asked and was informed of this fact at the last minute, given this information would have been communicated to him before US forces were in motion. In the days to come Trump would oscillate his messaging between saying he did not want war with Iran but that Tehran would be annihilated if war broke out; that his hawkish advisors were pushing for conflict; that he sought negotiations with no preconditions with Iran over its nuclear program; and that "If they [Iran] do something else, it'll [the US response] be double" (Borger and Wintour, 2019d). By most president's standards, such contradictory messaging would be unexpected; for Trump it is the norm.

The US drone strike that killed Iranian Major General Qasem Soleimani in Iraq on January 3, 2020, and that briefly seemed to place the region on the cusp of a US–Iran war, was also completely unpredictable, eliciting shock from much of the world (Wainer and Wadhams, 2020). It was at odds with the administration's – and the president's in particular – hesitance in responding to prior aggressive Iranian moves (and Trump's pledge in October 2019 to get the US out of "ridiculous Endless Wars" (@realDonaldTrump, October 7, 2019)) in the region with force, while risking a war seemed unwise as the US entered an election year. Yet, Trump still went through with the action, adding additional weight to his unpredictable bona fides.

So, has Trump's seeming irrationality paid off? It is very difficult to know – states, for obvious reasons, are loathe to admit they changed their policies/gave in to demands from others because the other was unpredictable and unnerved them. But it is notable that Iran's reaction to the Soleimani assassination was calculated to ensure it did not give cause for the US to escalate the situation into a larger war, as a warning was delivered hours ahead of time by Iran through Iraq to US forces that it intended to strike US military bases in Iraq (Ayash and Davison, 2020). Iran has also called Trump a "gambler" suggesting they view him as an unpredictable actor (Nadeau, 2020). On North Korea, Trump has ostensibly matched its unpredictability and, at times, bellicosity with his own. The fact negotiations have stalled and Pyongyang has stated that its self-imposed moratorium on nuclear and international ballistic missile testing has come to an end, but it has yet to restart testing, suggests they are wary of pushing the Trump administration too far. If sowing a sense of uncertainty in the minds of foreign leaders is the basic objective of this tactic, then Trump has definitely been successful.

Conclusion

This chapter has examined key components of the Trump administration's tactics. Evidence suggests that Trump, being a political and foreign policy outsider, has adopted tactics that suit his temperament and preferences and has drawn upon the negotiation skills he acquired from his pre-political career as a businessman. It made the case that Trump employs very high opening bids reflecting 'super aggressive expectations' that act as anchor positions, and a mixture of threats alongside promises of rewards. His threats to withdraw from multiple existing arrangements would, if enacted, likely damage US interests substantially. Yet, the threat to do so, which must be made plausible if

US negotiating partners or rogue regimes are to take the US seriously, is given credibility owing to Trump's behavior elsewhere. For example, Trump's withdrawal from the TPP and the Paris Agreement likely contributed to concerns in Mexico and Canada that the president's threat to abandon NAFTA was believable (spurring them to negotiate the USMCA), and also elevated concerns in NATO that he would remove the US from the alliance, increasing their incentives to enhance their contributions to the coalition. Trump's penchant to act unpredictably and seemingly irrationally – a tactic he has explicitly endorsed – means US negotiation partners cannot dismiss the 'Trump risk'; the president's behavior and rhetoric fits both his preferred negotiation style and his efforts to project an image of instability.

When we consider Trump's capricious behavior through the levels of analysis approach, the first level – Trump as an individual political actor – is illuminating. It accords not just with the Trump Doctrine outlined by senior officials but with Michael Pocalyko's contention that Trump's business education ensures he is comfortable operating amidst disruption and unpredictability (Pocalyko, 2017). Thus, to Trump, any disruption and favorable change of policy by US friends and adversaries merely "underscore core elements of his own policies" (Ibid., 53). However, President Nixon also consciously portrayed himself as a 'madman' to increase US leverage. As the next chapter explains, Nixon's presidential tenure took place during a period when the US faced immense international challenges and the emergence of a multipolar system – an international situation not unlike that facing Trump.

Trump clearly believes his pre-presidential approach is a model for success in the foreign policy domain. Has he been successful? The outcomes related to each of the four issues examined in this chapter suggest mixed results so far. On China a new Phase I deal was reached that addressed relatively 'low hanging fruit' and a framework for US–China trade negotiations now exists. However, securing a Phase II deal is expected to be extremely difficult and it is an open question whether the economic pain to the US (and global economy) from the trade war will ultimately be worth it. NAFTA was successfully renegotiated, leading to the USMCA (viewed by many as NAFTA-lite) that will provide small, albeit positive, gains for the US economy. Since Trump's inauguration, some of America's European NATO allies have increased their spending, which may be attributable to Trump's pressure, although Russia's aggression against Ukraine also certainly looms large in their calculations. Despite projections, the UK has kept its contributions at 2% of GDP. Contributions to the central budget were altered to suit US preferences but this is a small win given it involves only $2.5 billion of total spending. Some of the largest economies, such as France, Germany and Italy, have been stubborn in resisting US pressure, with Italy and France's defense spending decreasing since 2016, and Germany waiting until November 2019 to commit to increase its defense spending to 2% of GDP by 2031, asserting its decision was independent of the US president's pressure.

Finally, although no deal yet exists with North Korea and a new phase of escalation with Pyongyang is possible, North Korea has yet to return to long-range missile testing. In typical fashion, Trump has claimed success across all these issues, and, having got to this point by consistently employing a specific bargaining style alongside a penchant to act unpredictably, he will likely not alter his style of negotiating throughout the remainder of his presidency. Furthermore, the optics of a decisive president implementing his campaign promises to renegotiate 'unfair' deals undoubtedly plays well to Trump's domestic audience and that audience (especially his political base), trusting in his genius, are likely to stick with him even if his tactics do not bear substantial fruit.

Finally, Trump's pressure campaign, designed to extract concessions and improve America's national strength, is not inconsistent with the pressures that stem from the changing international structure: We could expect a great power, fearing the loss of its influence, to employ tactics to reduce the speed of its decline and attempt to position itself for a new period of dominance. The book now turns its attention to the system level of analysis to consider core elements of the Trump administration's strategy.

Notes

1 For a deeper discussion on this see Capehart (2015).
2 Although questions exist over how successful Trump's business operations are, in its 2019 billionaires ranking *Forbes* estimated President Trump's net worth at $3.1bn (Forbes, 2020). This includes multiple business interests and ventures (real estate, international hotels, casinos, golf courses, a variety of Trump branded and licensed products and licensing).
3 It is no accident that the charismatic minister Norman Vincent Peale, author of the 1950s bestseller *The Power of Positive Thinking*, married him and his first wife, Ivana (Shell, 2019, 41).
4 The president also sent a letter to Erdoğan on October 9, 2019, that contained all the basic elements of how he positions for negotiations. See Ho (2019).
5 Sam Roberts said Cohn was "beyond Machiavellian. He was an amazing manipulator", and Cohn's cousin, Roy Cohn, said "His lack of ethics, his lack of empathy ... for Roy life was transactional. It was all about accruing

connections and accruing power" (Tyrnauer, 2020). Cohn was prescient when he declared that "Donald Trump is probably one of the most important names in America today. What started off as a meteor, uh, mounting from New York and going upward is going to touch the rest of this country and good parts of the world. Donald just wants to be the biggest winner of all" (Ibid., 2020).

6 Along these lines Ivo H. Daalder and James M. Lindsay explain that the president received a briefing on July 20, 2017, in 'the tank' (one of the most secure facilities in the Pentagon) from senior foreign and national security officials. The officials sought to explain to the president the reason for America's outsized role in the world and why the liberal rules-based international order – including its alliances and trade agreements – benefited US national security and economic interests. Throughout the briefing Trump fired questions at his briefers, asking why US troops were in South Korea, why trade agreements did not provide trade surpluses for the US, and why Europe did not pay more towards NATO. Trump repeatedly replied, "I don't agree!" to the points the officials made and concluded the meeting by declaring that the rules-based order was "not working at all". He would also say to people after becoming president, "I inherited a mess" (Daalder and Lindsay, 2018, 2–3).

7 According to a *New York Times* article, Trump campaign advisors Sam Nunberg and Roger Stone in summer 2014 came up with the idea to tie his business experience as a builder to his anti-immigration proposals (Davis and Baker, 2019).

8 Ratification of the deal was held up in the US as Democrats negotiated with the administration to ensure it included tougher labor and environmental protections.

9 Although US engagement with NATO during the Trump era has not, technically, been through formal negotiations, the basic principles behind Trump's approach to negotiations apply.

10 Email exchange between Dr Steff and Dr Simona Soare (Senior Analyst at the European Union Institute for Security Studies).

Bibliography

@realDonaldTrump, November 29, 2011.
@realDonaldTrump, May 18, 2016.
@realDonaldTrump, October 19, 2016.
@realDonaldTrump, September 3, 2017.
@realDonaldTrump, March 2, 2018.
@realDonaldTrump, April 2, 2018.
@realDonaldTrump, July 12, 2018.
@realDonaldTrump, November 9, 2018.
@realDonaldTrump, December 9, 2018.
@realDonaldTrump, October 7, 2019.
@realDonaldTrump, October 8, 2019.
60 Minutes. Trump Gets Down to Business on 60 Minutes. 2015. Film.

Arms Control Association. Chronology of U.S.–North Korean Nuclear and Missile Diplomacy. July 2019. Retrieved from https://www.armscontrol.org/factsheets/dprkchron (accessed 12 October 2018).

Asia Times. N Korea Defends Nuclear Test Citing Fate of Saddam, Gaddafi. January 9, 2016. *Asia Times*. Retrieved from https://www.asiatimes.com/2016/01/article/n-korea-defends-nuclear-test-citing-fate-of-saddam-gaddafi/.

Ayash, Kamal, and John Davison. Hours of Forewarning Saved U.S., Iraqi Lives from Iran's Missile Attack. January 14, 2020. *Reuters*. Retrieved from https://www.reuters.com/article/us-iraq-security-early-warning/hours-of-forewarning-saved-u-s-iraqi-lives-from-irans-missile-attack-idUSKBN1ZC218.

Baker, Peter. Unpredictable as Ever, Trump Stuns with a Gamble on North Korea. March 11, 2018. *Sydney Morning Herald*. Retrieved from https://www.smh.com.au/world/asia/unpredictable-as-ever-trump-stuns-with-a-gamble-on-north-korea-20180311-p4z3tr.html.

Barnes, Julian, and Helene Cooper. Trump Discussed Pulling U.S. from NATO, Aides Say Amid New Concerns over Russia. January 14, 2019. *The New York Times*. Retrieved from https://www.nytimes.com/2019/01/14/us/politics/nato-president-trump.html.

BBC. North Korea 'Halts Missile and Nuclear Tests', Says Kim Jong-un. April 21, 2018. Retrieved from https://www.bbc.com/news/world-asia-43846488.

Benitez, Jorge. U.S. NATO Policy in the Age of Trump: Controversy and Consistency. Winter 2019. *The Fletcher Forum of World Affairs*, 31(1): 179–200.

Borger, Julian. Donald Trump: I'd Be Honored to Meet Kim Jong-Un Under 'Right Circumstances'. May 1, 2017. *The Guardian*. Retrieved from https://www.theguardian.com/us-news/2017/may/01/donald-trump-kim-jong-un-meeting-north-korea.

Borger, Julian, and Justin McCurry. North Korea Threatens to Cancel Trump Summit over Nuclear Demands. May 16, 2018. *The Guardian*. Retrieved from https://www.theguardian.com/world/2018/may/15/north-korea-talks-cancelled-trump-summit-latest.

Borger, Julian, and Benjamin Haas. Donald Trump Cancels North Korea Nuclear Summit. May 24, 2018. *The Guardian*. Retrieved from https://www.theguardian.com/us-news/2018/may/24/trump-cancels-north-korea-nuclear-summit.

Borger, Julian, and Anne Perkins. 'My Touch, My Feel': Trump Shows His Contempt for G7 Allies. June 9, 2018. *The Guardian*. Retrieved from https://www.theguardian.com/us-news/2018/jun/09/trump-g7-allies-comments-russia-north-korea.

Borger, Julian, and Patrick Wintour (a). US Says Video Shows Iranian Military Removing Mine from Tanker. June 14, 2019. *The Guardian*. Retrieved from https://www.theguardian.com/us-news/2019/jun/13/mike-pompeo-iran-gulf-oil-tanker-attacks.

Borger, Julian, and Patrick Wintour (b). Trump Suggests 'Loose and Stupid' Iranian Officer Attacked US Drone. June 21, 2019. *The Guardian*. Retrieved from https://www.theguardian.com/world/2019/jun.

Borger, Julian, and Wintour, Patrick (c). Trump Says He Stopped Airstrike on Iran because 150 would have Died. June 21, 2019. *The Guardian*. Retrieved from https://www.theguardian.com/world/2019/jun/21/donald-trump-retaliatory-iran-airstrike-cancelled-10-minutes-before.

Borger, Julian, and Patrick Wintour (d). Trump Says 'Absolutely Broken' Iran will Face Major New Sanctions. June 23, 2019. *The Guardian*. Retrieved from https://www.theguardian.com/world/2019/jun/23/iran-may-pull-further-away-from-nuclear-deal-after-latest-sanctions.

Breuninger, Kevin. Trump: Others Have to 'Figure the Situation Out' after US Announces Withdrawal from Northern Syria. 2019. *CNBC*. Retrieved from https://www.cnbc.com/2019/10/07/trump-other-countries-must-deal-with-isis-as-us-withdraws-from-northern-syria.html.

Browne, Ryan. Trump Administration to Cut its Financial Contribution to NATO. November 28, 2019. *CNN*. Retrieved from https://edition.cnn.com/2019/11/27/politics/trump-nato-contribution-nato/index.html.

Bryan, Bob, and Joseph Zeballos-Roig. Trump's New Major Trade Deal Looks a Lot Like NAFTA. Here are Key Differences between Them. December 10, 2019. *Markets Insider*. Retrieved from https://markets.businessinsider.com/news/stocks/us-canada-mexico-trade-deal-usmca-nafta-details-dairy-auto-dispute-resolution-2018-10-1027579947.

Buncombe, Andrew. Donald Trump's Explosive UN Speech: Read it in Full. September 19, 2017. *The Independent*. Retrieved from https://www.independent.co.uk/news/world/americas/us-politics/trump-un-speech-read-in-full-transcript-north-korea-general-assembly-a7956041.html.

Campbell, Charlie. President Trump Says China Could 'Easily' Rein in North Korea. November 9, 2017. *Time*. Retrieved from http://time.com/5016617/donald-trump-china-north-korea-2/.

Capehart, Kevin W. Hyman Minsky's Interpretation of Donald Trump. 2015. *Journal of Post Keynesian Economics*, 38(3): 477–492.

Chiacu, Doina, and Anthony Esposito. Trump Says May Tie Mexican Immigration Control to NAFTA. April 23, 2018. *Reuters*. Retrieved from https://www.reuters.com/article/us-trade-nafta-trump/trump-may-tie-mexican-immigration-control-to-nafta-idUSKBN1HU1ZE.

Cho, Youngwon. Method to the Madness of Chairman Kim: The Instrumental Rationality of North Korea's Pursuit of Nuclear Weapons. 2014. *International Journal*, 69(1): 5–25.

Chow, Daniel C.K. How the United States Uses the Trans-Pacific Partnership to Contain China in International Trade. 2016. *Chicago Journal of International Law*, 12(2): 370–402.

Cranley, Allen. From $1.6 Million to $1.1 Billion: How Much the 10 Wealthiest Members of Trump's Cabinet are Worth. January 11, 2019. *Business Insider*. Retrieved from https://amp.thisisinsider.com/trump-cabinet-members-net-worth-2019-1.

Cummings, William. 'Trump Is Having an Impact': NATO Head Credits President's Tough Talk for $100B boost. January 27, 2019. *USA Today*.

Retrieved from https://www.usatoday.com/story/news/world/2019/01/27/nato-chief-credits-trump/2695799002/.

Daalder, Ivo H., and James M. Lindsay. *The Empty Throne: America's Abdication of Global Leadership.* New York: Public Affairs, 2018.

Dai, Xinyuan. Who Defines the Rules of the Game in East Asia? The Trans-Pacific Partnership and the Strategic Use of International Institutions. 2015. *International Relations of the Asia-Pacific,* 15(1): 1–25.

Davis, Julie, and Peter Baker. How the Border Wall is Boxing Trump In. January 5, 2019. *New York Times.* Retrieved from https://www.nytimes.com/2019/01/05/us/politics/donald-trump-border-wall.html.

Denyer, Simon, and Min Joo Kim. In South Korea, Military Cost Dispute and Trump's Moves in Syria Fuel Doubts over U.S. Commitment. November 5, 2019. *The Washington Post.* Retrieved from https://www.washingtonpost.com/world/asia_pacific/in-south-korea-military-cost-dispute-and-trumps-moves-in-syria-fuel-doubts-over-us-commitment/2019/11/01/7048b030-fa30-11e9-9534-e0dbcc9f5683_story.html.

Donnan, Shawn. The Tough Negotiator Turning Trump's Trade Bluster into Reality. 2018. *Bloomberg.* Retrieved from https://www.bloomberg.com/news/articles/2018-09-20/the-tough-negotiator-turning-trump-s-trade-bluster-into-reality.

Emmott, Robin. Germany Commits to NATO Spending Goal by 2031 for First Time. November 8, 2019. *Reuters.* https://www.reuters.com/article/us-germany-nato/germany-commits-to-nato-spending-goal-by-2031-for-first-time-idUSKBN1XH1IK.

Farley, Robert. Is Mexico Paying for the Wall Through USMCA? December 14, 2018. *FactCheck.org.* Retrieved from https://www.factcheck.org/2018/12/is-mexico-paying-for-the-wall-through-usmca/.

Fathi, Nazila. Wipe Israel 'Off the Map' Iranian Says. October 25, 2005. *New York Times.* Retrieved from https://www.nytimes.com/2005/10/27/world/africa/wipe-israel-off-the-map-iranian-says.html.

Forbes. The Definitive Networth of Donald Trump. 2020. Retrieved from https://www.forbes.com/donald-trump/.

Fox News. Donald Trump says America Has to Be 'Less Predictable'. November 3, 2015. *YouTube.* Retrieved from https://www.youtube.com/watch?v=mfrfrHLQWYk.

Garcia, Feliks. Donald Trump Foreign Policy Speech: 5 Contradictions in the Presidential Hopeful's Plan. April 28, 2016. *The Independent.* Retrieved from https://www.independent.co.uk/news/world/americas/donald-trump-foreign-policy-speech-5-contradictions-in-the-presidential-hopefuls-plan-a7005711.html.

Goldberg, Jeffrey. A Senior White House Official Defines the Trump Doctrine: 'We're America, Bitch'. June 11, 2018. *The Atlantic.* Retrieved from https://www.theatlantic.com/politics/archive/2018/06/a-senior-white-house-official-defines-the-trump-doctrine-were-america-bitch/562511/.

Herszenhorn, David M. NATO Spending Tweak Lets Berlin Push Back on Trump. November 11, 2019. *Politico*. Retrieved from https://www.politico.eu/article/nato-spending-tweak-lets-berlin-take-on-trump/.

Hickey, C.K. NATO Defense Funds Have Been Building for Years, but Trump Wants the Credit. December 3, 2019. *Foreign Policy*. Retrieved from https://foreignpolicy.com/2019/12/03/nato-defense-funds-have-been-building-for-years-but-trump-wants-the-credit/.

Ho, Vivian. Donald Trump's Bizarre, Threatening Letter to Erdoğan: 'Don't Be a Fool'. October 17, 2019. *The Guardian*. Retrieved from https://www.theguardian.com/us-news/2019/oct/16/trump-letter-erdogan-turkey-invasion.

Horsley, Scott. Trump Signs 'Phase 1' China Trade Deal, but Most Tariffs Remain in Place. January 15, 2020. *NPR*. Retrieved from https://www.npr.org/2020/01/15/796305300/trump-to-sign-phase-one-china-trade-deal-but-most-tariffs-remain-in-place.

Johnson, Jesse. North Korea's Kim Warns of 'New Strategic Weapon' as Nuclear Freeze Falters. January 1, 2020. *Japan Times*. Retrieved from https://www.japantimes.co.jp/news/2020/01/01/asia-pacific/politics-diplomacy-asia-pacific/kim-warns-new-strategic-weapon-north-korea-snubs-arms-test-moratorium-face-gangster-like-u-s/#.XjZ0KWgzY2w.

Kaufman, Joyce P. The US Perspective on NATO under Trump: Lessons of the Past and Prospects for the Future. 2017. *International Affairs*, 93(2): 251–266.

Khrushcheva, Nina L. The Return of the Madman Theory. October 5, 2017. *Japan Times*. Retrieved from https://www.japantimes.co.jp/opinion/2017/10/05/commentary/world-commentary/return-madman-theory/#.XTd4augzaUk.

Kogan, Eugene B. Art of the Power Deal: The Four Negotiation Roles of Donald J. Trump. 2019. *Negotiation Journal*, 35(1): 65–83.

Kranish, M., and M. Fisher. *Trump Revealed: The Definitive Biography of the 45th President*. New York: Scribner, 2016.

Laderman, Charlie, and Brendan Simms. *Donald Trump: The Making of a World View*. New York: I.B. Tauris, 2017.

Masters, James, and Katie Hunt. Trump Rattles NATO with 'Obsolete' Blast. January 17, 2016. *CNN*. Retrieved from https://www.cnn.com/2017/01/16/politics/donald-trump-times-bild-interview-takeaways/index.html.

Masterson, Julia. Chronology of U.S.–North Korean Nuclear and Missile Diplomacy. January 2020. *Arms Control Association*. Retrieved from https://www.armscontrol.org/factsheets/dprkchron.

McCurry, Justin. Military Action against North Korea 'An Option,' Warns Rex Tillerson. March 17, 2017. *The Guardian*. Retrieved from https://www.theguardian.com/us-news/2017/mar/17/military-action-against-north-korea-an-option-warns-rex-tillerson.

Nadeau, Barbie Latza. Adviser to Iran's Supreme Leader Warns of 'Military' Response. January 5, 2020. *The Daily Beast*. Retrieved from https://www.thedailybeast.com/iran-supreme-leader-ayatollah-khameneis-adviser-warns-of-military-response-over-qassem-soleimani-killing.

Naftalo, Tim. The Problem with Trump's Madman Theory. October 4, 2017. *The Atlantic*. Retrieved from https://www.theatlantic.com/international/archive/2017/10/madman-theory-trump-north-korea/542055/.

Nakamura, David, and Gearan, Anne. U.S. Warns that Time Is Running Out for Peaceful Solution with North Korea. September 17, 2017. *The Washington Post*. Retrieved from https://www.washingtonpost.com/politics/us-warns-that-time-is-running-out-for-peaceful-solution-with-north-korea/2017/09/17/101dcdea-9bd6-11e7-8ea1-ed975285475e_story.html.

NATO. Defense Expenditure of NATO Countries (2013–2019). November 29, 2019. https://www.nato.int/nato_static_fl2014/assets/pdf/pdf_2019_11/20191129_pr-2019-123-en.pdf.

Navarro, Peter. *The Coming China Wars: Where They Will Be Fought and How They Can Be Won*. Upper Saddle River, NJ: Pearson Education, 2007.

Navarro, Peter, and Greg Autry. *Death by China: Confronting the Dragon – A Global Call to Action*. Upper Saddle River, NJ: Pearson FT Press, 2011.

Parker, Ashley. Trump Willing to Break Up NATO. April 4, 2016. *New York Times*. Retrieved from https://www.atlanticcouncil.org/blogs/natosource/trump-willing-to-break-up-nato. (accessed July 24, 2019).

Pocalyko, Michael. The Businessman President. 2017. *Survival*, 59(1): 51–57.

Politico. Full transcript: Donald Trump's Jobs Plan Speech. June 28, 2016. *Politico*. Retrieved from https://www.politico.com/story/2016/06/full-transcript-trump-job-plan-speech-224891.

Pramuk, Jacob. Trump Warns North Korea Threats 'Will Be Met with Fire and Fury'. August 8, 2017. *CNBC*. Retrieved from https://www.cnbc.com/2017/08/08/trump-warns-north-korea-threats-will-be-met-with-fire-and-fury.html.

Qiu, Linda. Is Donald Trump's *Art of the Deal* the Best-selling Business Book of all Time? July 6, 2015. *Politifact*. Retrieved from https://www.politifact.com/truth-o-meter/statements/2015/jul/06/donald-trump/donald-trumps-art-deal-best-selling-business-book-/.

Raynova, Denitsa, and Ian Kearns. The Wales Pledge Revisited: A Preliminary Analysis of 2015 Budget Decisions in NATO Member States. February 2015. *European Leadership Network*. Retrieved from https://www.europeanleadershipnetwork.org/wp-content/uploads/2017/10/ELN-NATO-Budgets-Brief.pdf.

Rathbun, Brian. Does Structure Trump All? A Test of Agency in World Politics. In (eds.) Jervis, Robert, et al. *Chaos in the Liberal Order: The Trump Presidency and International Politics in the Twenty-First Century*. New York: Columbia University Press, 2018.

Restuccia, Andrew. Trump and Xi Compete to Lay on the Highest Praise in Beijing. November 11, 2017. *Politico*. Retrieved from https://www.politico.com/story/2017/11/09/trump-china-trade-deficit-244728.

Reuters. Department of Commerce Bans U.S. Firms from Selling to ZTE for 7 years. April 16, 2018. *Venturebeat*. Retrieved from https://venturebeat.com/2018/04/16/department-of-commerce-bans-u-s-firms-from-selling-to-zte-for-7-years/.

Sagan, Scott D., and Jeremi Suri. The Madman Nuclear Alert: Secrecy, Signaling, and Safety in October 1969. 2003. *International Security*, 27(4): 150–183.

Schelling, Thomas C. *Arms and Influence.* New Haven, CT: Yale University Press, 1966.

Schelling, Thomas C. *The Strategy of Conflict* (2nd ed.). Cambridge, MA: Harvard University Press, 1981.

Sechser, Todd S., and Fuhrmann, Mathew. Policy Series: The Madman Myth: Trump and the Bomb. March 22, 2017. *H-Diplo|ISSF POLICY Series.* Retrieved from https://issforum.org/roundtables/policy/1-5w-madman.

Shell, G. Richard. Transactional Man: Teaching Negotiation Strategy in the Age of Trump. 2019. *Negotiation Journal*, 35(1): 31–45.

Steff, Reuben. The Audacity of Trump: How He Won and What We Missed. 2017. *New Zealand International Review*, 42(2): 2–5.

Stracqualursi, Veronica. 10 Times Trump Attacked China and its Trade Relations with the US. November 9, 2017. *ABC News*. Retrieved from https://abcnews.go.com/Politics/10-times-trump-attacked-china-trade-relations-us/story?id=46572567.

Swan, Jonathan. Scoop: Trump Urges Staff to Portray Him as 'Crazy Guy'. October 2, 2017. *Axios*. Retrieved from https://www.axios.com/scoop-trump-urges-staff-to-portray-him-as-crazy-guy-1513305888-c1cbdb89-6370-4e13-98ed-28c414e62a35.html.

Tenpas, Kathryn Dunn, Elaine Kamarck, and Nicholas W. Zeppos. Tracking Turnover in the Trump Administration. November 7, 2018. *Brookings*. Retrieved from https://www.brookings.edu/research/tracking-turnover-in-the-trump-administration/.

Time. Here's Donald Trump's Presidential Announcement Speech, June 16, 2015. Retrieved from https://time.com/3923128/donald-trump-announcement-speech/.

Time. Read Donald Trump's Speech on Trade. June 28, 2016. Retrieved from http://time.com/4386335/donald-trump-trade-speech-transcript/.

Trump, Donald, and Dave Shiflett. *The America We Deserve.* Los Angeles: Renaissance Books, 2000.

Trump, Donald, and Schwartz, Tony. *Trump: The Art of the Deal*, New York: Ballantine Books, 2015 edition.

Tun-Jen, Cheng, and Peter C.Y. Chow. The TPP and the Pivot: Economic and Security Nexus. In (ed.) Chow, P.C.Y. *The US Strategic Pivot to Asia and Cross-Strait Relations.* New York: Palgrave Macmillan, 2014.

Turak, Natasha. Iran Shoots down American Drone in International Airspace in 'Unprovoked Attack,' US Says. June 20, 2019. *CNBC*. Retrieved from https://www.cnbc.com/2019/06/20/us-drone-shot-down-by-iranian-missile-in-international-airspace.html.

Tyrnauer, Matt. Where's My Roy Cohn? 2020. Sony Pictures Classics.

UBS/PwC. Billionaire: Masters Architects of Great Wealth and Lasting Legacies. 2015. Retrieved from https://www.pwc.com/gx/en/financial-services/publications/assets/pwc-ubs-billionaire-report.pdf.

United States International Trade Commission. USITC Releases Report Concerning the Likely Impact of the United States–Mexico–Canada Agreement (USMCA). 2019. Retrieved from https://www.usitc.gov/press_room/news_release/2019/er0418ll1087.htm.

US Trade Representative. Economic and Trade Agreement between the Government of the United States of America and the Government of the People's Republic of China. 2020. Retrieved from https://ustr.gov/sites/default/files/files/agreements/phase%20one%20agreement/Economic_And_Trade_Agreement_Between_The_United_States_And_China_Text.pdf.

Wainer, David, and Nick Wadhams. U.S. Killing of Soleimani Leaves Trump 'Totally Unpredictable'. January 4, 2020. *Bloomberg*. Retrieved from https://www.bloomberg.com/news/articles/2020-01-04/u-s-killing-of-soleimani-leaves-trump-totally-unpredictable.

Westcott, Ben. What the US and North Korea Mean When they Talk about 'Denuclearization'. June 11, 2018. *CNN*. Retrieved from https://edition.cnn.com/2018/05/23/asia/what-is-denuclearization-north-korea-intl/index.html.

White House (a). Remarks by President Trump at NATO Unveiling of the Article 5 and Berlin Wall Memorials – Brussels, Belgium. May 25, 2017. Retrieved from https://www.whitehouse.gov/briefings-statements/remarks-president-trump-nato-unveiling-article-5-berlin-wall-memorials-brussels-belgium/.

White House (b). Remarks by President Trump on the Administration's National Security Strategy. December 18, 2017. Retrieved from https://www.whitehouse.gov/briefings-statements/remarks-president-trump-administrations-national-security-strategy/.

White House. Joint Statement of President Donald J. Trump of the United States of America and Chairman Kim Jong Un of the Democratic People's Republic of Korea at the Singapore Summit. June 12, 2018. Retrieved from https://www.whitehouse.gov/briefings-statements/joint-statement-president-donald-j-trump-united-states-america-chairman-kim-jong-un-democratic-peoples-republic-korea-singapore-summit/.

Wong, Dorcas, and Alexander Chipman Koty. The US–China Trade War: A Timeline. January 29, 2019. *China Briefing*. Retrieved from https://www.china-briefing.com/news/the-us-china-trade-war-a-timeline/.

4 The systemic challenges of multipolarity

The trials and tribulations of a Kissingerian grand strategy

Introduction

The discussions in Chapters 2 and 3 have assumed that the Trump administration's foreign policy settings originate with the man, and to a lesser extent relate to domestic considerations. An alternative frame for comparison used in this chapter holds that rather than being a peculiarity of Trump, key aspects of contemporary US policy reflect long-standing systemic challenges, specifically the structural trend towards multipolarity. While these forces existed and influenced US foreign policy during the Obama administration,[1] the Trump administration has taken it further by overtly adopting and championing Kissingerian realist principles. In this, realpolitik and flexibility play key roles in efforts to maximize US power and influence in an international system comprised of numerous great powers. By making this case, the chapter provides a rationale for aspects of Trump's foreign policy that are fiercely contested, arguing that it relates to structural factors – Trump is leaving a personal stamp in a way supported by structural forces. However, while President Trump's rhetoric in this area has diverged from that of past presidents', suggestive of a genuine desire to alter US foreign policy, its substance has not significantly shifted across many issues due to bureaucratic opposition in the establishment.

The chapter consists of seven sections. The first explains that the perceptible relative shift in power away from America is resulting in a more competitive multipolar international arena, akin to that which confronted the Nixon–Kissinger administration (indeed, Henry Kissinger acts as a personal link between the Kissinger and Trump administrations, and appears to have made a mark on the latter's policy) leading the Trump administration to emphasize material interests and a Kissingerian foreign policy that eschews liberal ideology. The second advances this discussion to consider how the rise of China primes Washington and

Beijing to seek out partners to magnify their existing positions, a task the third section explains is made more challenging given Washington's post-Cold War strategy of liberal hegemony. This held the objective of transforming the world in America's image but, ultimately, damaged US power and influence in the process, accelerating the return of multipolarity. As such, systemic forces compel the US to dispense with aggressively promoting liberalism and democracy in world affairs, since this ideological impulse reduces the flexibility of its foreign policy and leaves it disadvantaged in its competition with China. The fourth extends the analysis to the triangle of relations between the US, Russia, and China. Here, structural forces generate incentives for Washington to seek to improve ties with Moscow to shift the balance of power away from China. The fifth shows how efforts to act on these demands were derailed by 'the Blob' – a group of institutions and bureaucratic actors that make up the foreign policy establishment. If an anti-China coalition of mixed liberal and authoritarian regimes is necessary to check China's global ambitions, the Blob may very well constitute the most significant force that prevents its emergence. The sixth section considers whether a Kissingerian strategy has produced discernible benefits in US relations with authoritarian states and America's European NATO allies. The seventh and concluding section explains that a structural lens provides insights into the Trump administration's strategy, although it does not explain the president's method of advancing that strategy which, so far, appears to have undermined it.

Multipolarity and a Kissingerian strategy

Prior to and during his time in office Donald Trump has displayed indifference towards liberal values and US exceptionalism. This manifested in a number of ways:[2] he has repeatedly criticized US allies for not pulling their weight; refused initially to endorse America's commitment to NATO's Article 5 guarantee during his first trip to Europe; threatened to walk away from the KORUS agreement with South Korea; and ignored human rights violations by Russia, Myanmar, Turkey, and China. Trump also showed his contempt for the liberal order when he arrived at the Group of Seven (G7) meeting in June 2018 late and left one day early.[3] At the meeting he called for Russia to be readmitted to the group, while the US delegation ensured that the word liberal was removed from the final communiqué document and the rules-based order was referred to as 'a' rules-based order rather than 'the' rules-based order. Even then, after the communiqué was released, Trump rejected his endorsement (BBC, 2018). Furthermore, Freedom House's 2018 and 2019 reports explain that while the Obama administration defended democratic principles in its foreign policy statements, the Trump administration, in both word and deed, has explicitly cast off democratic principles as a guide for US policy amidst a sustained 13-year decline in democratic freedoms worldwide (Freedom House, 2018, 2019).

In contrast to his treatment of America's liberal allies, Trump is outwardly friendly towards authoritarian leaders of what Freedom House characterizes as 'not free' or 'partly free' regimes (Freedom House, 2018). One explanation for this is that he seeks to erode American checks and balances in order to centralize power in the executive branch; the president sees something he recognizes and respects in 'strongmen' offshore, whether it is Philippine President Rodrigo Duterte, Russian President Vladimir Putin, China's President Xi Jinping, Turkey's President Recep Erdoğan or North Korean leader Kim Jong-un – all of whom he has praised at one time or another (Steff, 2018).[4] In keeping with the theme of this chapter, this section argues that a system-level explanation exists for Trump's rhetoric towards autocratic actors. Essentially, the shifting balance of power towards multipolarity and return of great power competition with China compels Washington to adopt a Kissingerian foreign policy that is less interventionist and more flexible, able to work with states irrespective of regime type.

Randall Schweller proposes that the Trump administration's foreign policy is largely a response to forces generated at the international level (Schweller, 2018a, 2018b, 2018c); US influence has waned due to the flawed strategy of liberal hegemony Washington pursued after 1991 and that found its fullest (and most disastrous) expression during the George W. Bush administration. John Mearsheimer agrees with this assessment, saying that rather than empower the US, this strategy failed since it was pursued "at the expense of balance of power politics", i.e. realism, and was only permitted by a unipolar system in which the US confronted no significant threat from other great powers (Mearsheimer, 2019, 1). Relatedly, Taesuh Cha and Jungkun Seo make a compelling case that Trump's foreign policy echoes the Nixon administration's emphasis on the national (predominantly material) interest. Much like Nixon, Trump presides over the executive at a time of relative US decline and domestic political polarization. These factors do not just create a domestic political environment conducive to the election of political mavericks, such as Nixon and Trump, but also generate incentives for "an unconventional course of realpolitik in world politics", and "dramatic shifts in policies … to ensure that the United States will remain a hegemonic power on the world scene" (Cha and Seo, 2018, 80).

Nixon and Kissinger were dealing with the Vietnam quagmire, Soviet establishment of nuclear parity, the rise of Japan's economy and a global recession that threatened the US-led economic order. As such, Henry Kissinger wrote that "a major reassessment of American foreign policy" (Ibid., 81) was necessary, including reorienting towards a narrow emphasis on US national interests and realist concepts where the US would balance its competitors against one another. In this context, American exceptionalism as a guide to US behavior had to be set aside – it would reduce America's foreign policy flexibility. Along these lines, Nixon said at the 1969 NATO summit that "Those who think simply in terms of 'good' nations and 'bad' nations – of a world of staunch allies and sworn enemies – live in a world of their own" (Ibid., 84). Greater flexibility facilitated the administration's efforts to set aside China's Communist ideology and authoritarian regime as a pertinent factor in US–China relations. In doing so, Washington was able to exploit tensions in the Sino–Soviet Alliance (1950–1979) that escalated into a seven-month border war in 1969 (Kuisong, 2000), shifting the global balance in America's favor at the expense of the Soviet Union which posed a greater threat at that time to the US than China.

As Trump faces a set of systemic challenges similar to those of the Nixon administration, Cha and Seo suggest we are seeing a "Kissingerian grand strategy redux" (Cha and Seo, 2018, 86). Consider the situation that faced the US at the start of the Trump presidency in January 2017: a noted decline of US influence in the wake of a decade of US overstretch in the Middle East, a loss of faith in the US-led global economic order as a result of the 2008 financial crisis, and the rise of the BRICs (Brazil, Russia, India, and China), especially China, and the resurgence of Russia. This signals the arrival of multipolarity. As such, George Friedman writes that in a similar vein to Kissinger's quote above, the newly installed president proposed "a redefinition of U.S. foreign policies based on current realities, not those of 40 years ago. It is a foreign policy in which American strength is maximized in order to achieve American ends" (Friedman, 2017). The administration's preference for bilateralism is also understandable as a response to these structural forces: It frees the US from multilateral restraints that require the US to take into account collective interests – a principle at odds with the core sentiment of 'America *first*' and prevents the US bringing its superior material powers to bear in its foreign relations. To the Trump administration, multilateralism acts to level the playing field between large and small states, allowing others to 'gang up' on the United States. Consider that when commenting on the TPP, Trump said "It would give up all of our economic leverage to an international commission ... We need bilateral trade deals. We do not need to enter into another massive international agreement that ties us up and binds us down, like TPP does" (Time, 2016). At other times he stated "I like bilateral [negotiations], because if you have a problem, you terminate. When you're in with many countries ... you don't have that same option" and "When you get into the mosh pit ... with all these countries together, you can't get out of the deal. And you take the lowest denominator" (Kogan, 2019, 75).

According to Trump, recent US foreign policy was driven by the "foolishness and arrogance" of a misguided foreign policy elite that sought to be the "policeman of the world" (Cha and Seo, 2018, 85, 88). In contrast, he dubbed his administration's approach 'Principled Realism' during his address to the UN General Assembly in 2017 (Trump, 2017b). The 2017 *National Security Strategy* (2017 NSS) explained this policy: "It is realist because it acknowledges the central role of power in international politics, affirms that sovereign states are the best hope for a peaceful world, and clearly defines our national interests. It is principled because it is grounded in the knowledge that advancing American principles spreads peace and prosperity around the globe. We are guided by our values and disciplined by our interests" (White House, 2017, 55). In a speech to the Claremont Institute on May 11, 2019, Secretary of State Mike Pompeo declared the essence of the administration's foreign policy to be "realism, restraint, and respect" (Pompeo, 2019a). Pompeo criticized post-Cold War US foreign policy for putting undue faith in international organizations and the "so-called rules-based international order", noting America's leaders "had drifted from realism" and that "taking the pursuit of America's interests up a notch is not just honorable; it's urgent in this new era of great power competition" (Ibid.). While he criticized America's authoritarian competitors, such as Russia, China, Iran and North Korea, he also said America "has no aspiration to use force to spread the American model. You can see it in the administration's record of its using force" (Ibid.).

The next section advances this discussion, explaining how the rise of China primes Washington and Beijing to seek out partners to enhance their existing positions and prevent states from not leaning towards or strategically aligning with the other great power.

The China challenge

In terms of material power, soft power, and the ability to compete ideologically (by offering an alternative model of authoritarian capitalism to US liberal capitalism) China is the only conceivable near-peer contender to America's position in the 21st century (Brooks and

Wohlforth, 2015/2016; Rolland, 2020). Military and economic statistics illustrate the growth in China's relative power: in 1994 the US accounted for roughly one-fourth of world GDP and 40% of global military spending; by 2015 it accounted for 22.4% of world GDP and 33.8% of global military spending. In comparison, China accounted for 3.3% of the world GDP in 1994 and 2.2% of global military spending, by 2015 these figures rose to 11.8% of global GDP and 12.2% of world military spending (Brands, 2018, 11–12). Estimates for 2019 indicate the US economy accounted for 24.8% of world GDP compared to China with 16.3%, and US military spending in 2018 was 36% of the global total and China's 14% (IMF, 2019; SIPRI, 2019, 2). In aggregate, this has led China down the path to where it is now an "emerging potential superpower" (Brooks and Wohlforth, 2015/2016, 43) that is not just an economic competitor to Washington, but a military one able to challenge the balance of military power across the Asia-Pacific through its development of Anti-Access/Area-Denial capabilities and militarization of the South China Seas (O'Rourke, 2020; Allison, 2020). China's influence is also increasingly global owing to its determined efforts to expand its influence into South America, Africa, and Asia and establish multilateral institutions that challenge the existing set of global economic and security institutions established by the US in the wake of World War II (Clarke, 2017).

Are concerns over China's rise exaggerated? Schweller makes the case that America and China's "two nationalisms pose no inherent conflict of interests" (Schweller, 2018a, 25), since China desires more global influence and the US less. Fareed Zakaria has argued that misreading the extent and nature of the Chinese challenge risks producing policies that make the situation worse (Zakaria, 2020). However, voices like this urging caution are increasingly scarce in Washington DC. Robert Kaplan's view of the competition is characteristic of a much more prevalent sentiment. Kaplan contends that the "differences between the United States and China are stark and fundamental ... The philosophical divide between the American and Chinese systems is becoming as great as the gap between American democracy and Soviet communism" (Kaplan, 2019). Additionally, the security dilemma dynamics between Washington and Beijing (Steff and Khoo, 2017; Johnson, 2018) have gone largely unaddressed, and politically there is a unified Democrat–Republican front against China's rise and expanding global ambitions that's also reflected in DC's constellation of foreign policy-focused think tanks.

Throughout the mounting US–China competition, the US will naturally seek to ensure that as many states as possible maintain their strategic distance from Beijing and lean towards Washington. This is a task that will become more difficult as China's power rises and the US finds it harder to reassure its allies and partners that it can maintain its military dominance (Graaff and Apeldoorn, 2018; Friedberg, 2018; Layne, 2018; Mazarr, Heath, and Cevallos, 2018), while non-aligned states may feel compelled to move towards China. In short, the ongoing power shift means a number of states throughout the Asia-Pacific and Eurasia are 'up for grabs' as they hedge their position between the existent hegemon and the rising challenger (Jackson, 2014; Lind, 2018; Horton, 2019; Mearsheimer, 2019). And while China has an official policy of not seeking outright allies – a fact that might re-assure Western officials they have advantage in retaining and se-curing allies against China – a debate is underway in China that could lead Beijing to alter or abandon this policy (Ruonan and Fend, 2017).

In this context, John Mearsheimer predicts three 'realist orders' will emerge. The first will be a thin one, where international in-stitutions manage aspects of global economic and military activities that overlaps two 'bounded orders' – one dominated and led by the US, the other centered on China. These US and China orders will be held together by military alliances and engage in significant eco-nomic and military competition with one another. Ultimately, the US–China rivalry will "bear a marked resemblance to the three Cold War orders, albeit with China taking the place of the Soviet Union" (Mearsheimer, 2019, 45). The period between now and the formation of these US and China-led orders will see intense jostling between Washington and Beijing for partners and (official or de facto) allies. A number of states relevant to the mounting US–China strategic competition have authoritarian governance systems and/or forms of illiberal democracy, while more have trended in this di-rection over the past decade (Freedom House, 2018, 2019). As such, a growing number of states do not share America's governing lib-eral ideology – a fact that could complicate America's efforts to keep these out of China's orbit, especially as Beijing claims it has no interest in the domestic affairs of other countries, nor does not seek to spread or impose its ideology beyond its borders (Wintour, 2015). Some evidence supports this as Beijing does not condition its aid and support for regimes depending upon whether they are author-itarian or democratic (Givens, 2011). This state of affairs could leave the US at a disadvantage in its competition with China. Considering the recent historical context sheds light on this and provides a more thorough explanation as to why a shift away from liberal hegemony gained currency in the Trump administration.

The failure of liberal enlargement

Throughout the Cold War the US confronted an existential competitor in the Soviet Union. In the face of this, the objective of spreading liberalism was often set aside in favor of strategic interests. Yet, as unipolarity emerged after the Cold War, it offered Washington seemingly immense discretion and freedom to indulge its ideological impulses. Consequently, the objective of promoting liberalism became one of the key drivers of US foreign policy. Firstly, the Clinton administration announced in 1993 "The successor to a doctrine of containment must be a strategy of enlargement, enlargement of the world's free community of market democracies" (Friedman, 1993). Then the drive to spread democracy became militarized in response to the catalytic event of 9/11 and the Bush administration's announcement of a global 'War on Terror'. In turn, offensive liberalism shifted to the forefront of US grand strategy, which had become increasingly ideological (Miller, 2010). Rather than act like a status quo power, America's response to 9/11 was to act as a revolutionary one by using its influence to try to change the international system in its own image in the belief that the only way for the US to be safe was for liberalism and democracy to triumph everywhere. This would usher in a global democratic peace (the absence of conflict between mature democracies) (Russett, 1993; Jervis, 2003; Desch, 2007/2008; Jervis, 2009) entailing an activist foreign policy that included ideology promotion and commitment to perpetual American military dominance, as the administration became a forceful proponent of democratic ideals and of the need to expand democracy to unstable regions through Bush's Freedom Agenda (Bush, 2010, 395–439). This was enshrined in the 2002 NSS, which identified a "single sustainable model of national success: freedom, democracy and free enterprise" (White House, 2002, i). In the eyes of the Bush administration, illiberal regimes were fundamentally illegitimate and liberal hegemony was a grand strategy that would maximize American ability to achieve its objectives.

Bush appeared to offer states a stark choice in November 2001 when he declared, "You're either with us or against us in the fight against terror" (CNN, 2001). After the US toppled the Taliban regime in Afghanistan, a starker display of the administration's agenda occurred when the US invaded Iraq – a state that was not involved in the 9/11 attacks – in March 2003, part of what Bush called a "global democratic revolution" (Barbash, 2003). Explaining US objectives, General Wesley Clark said that Iraq was envisaged as the beginning of a five-year campaign targeting seven countries (including Iraq, Syria, Lebanon, Libya, Iran, Somalia, and Sudan) (Clark, 2003, 130).

Naturally, many other illiberal states beyond these likely felt they had cause to fear US power and intentions, especially after the US invaded Afghanistan and Iraq, making it clear force would be used to enact regime change and 'spread' America's liberal ideology. Presumably, the Bush administration thought that by showing America's capacity to invade Iraq and depose Saddam Hussein, it would send a clear signal to other illiberal regimes that aligning with the US was essential not just to their national interests, but potentially to their survival. Some states appeared to receive this message. For example, Libya, led by Muammar Gaddafi, agreed to give up its Weapons of Mass Destruction (WMD) in exchange for being welcomed back into the international community (Jentleson and Whytock, 2005/2006; Hochman, 2006; Leverett, 2007). Yet these steps did not prevent a US and NATO-led effort to support a rebel uprising against him in 2011, ultimately leading to regime change.

As the US–China competition advances to take center stage in international relations, the above context continues to have resonance for states calculating their options. Consider, what could encourage these states in the emerging US–China competition to lean towards China? Firstly, they may view US power in and of itself as a threat. However, states do not just balance power – they balance threat (Walt, 1987), which includes assessing whether another state has offensive *intentions* towards them. This speaks to a second key point: The American impulse to spread liberalism through a liberal hegemonic grand strategy – evident in the record of offensive action against illiberal regimes in the post-Cold War era – could drive states into perpetual competition with the US and towards a China-led security order. Not free (authoritarian) or partly free regimes could come to believe that if Washington considers liberal democracies the only sustainable models of success and candidates for partnership, and the US has a historical mission to transform the world in its image, then America's offensive stance towards them is permanent. Beijing, claiming to have no ideological intentions to transform the world in its image, reduces concerns that it has latent offensive intent against these states. As such, illiberal regimes may be safer in dealing with and trusting the Chinese government – enhancing the prospects they will decide to join a China-led order. Statements by President Trump and his top officials that the US does not seek to impose its way of life by force or condition on its foreign partnerships on ideological grounds takes on a new light in this context, enhancing the prospects authoritarian states will align with Washington over Beijing.

Managing China's rise and the US–Russia–China strategic triangle

A key geopolitical nexus that could decisively influence the global balance of power is the strategic triangle of relations between the US, Russia, and China. The 2017 NSS and 2018 *National Defense Strategy* (2018 NDS) make clear that the "central challenge to U.S. prosperity and security is the re-emergence of long-term, strategic competition" with China and Russia which are both considered "revisionist powers … trying to change the international order in their favor" (White House, 2017, 25; Department of Defense, 2018, 2). While Moscow is called out for its belligerent and disruptive behavior, the NDS considers China to be America's greatest long-term challenge, asserting that Beijing is enacting a "military modernization program that seeks Indo-Pacific regional hegemony in the near-term and displacement of the United States to achieve global pre-eminence in the future" (Department of Defense, 2018, 2).

In an increasingly competitive multipolar environment, the structural logic behind improving US–Russian relations serves the objective of prising Moscow away from its drift towards China, eliminating the prospect of a strong China and Russian entente emerging. Here, the balance of threat comes into play. Mearsheimer explains that while he believes Russia is "now aligned with China", if Moscow *fears* China more than the US it will loosely integrate into the "U.S.-led bounded order" (Mearsheimer, 2019, 48). However, if it continues to deepen its relationship with China because it fears Washington more than Beijing, it will loosely integrate into the Chinese order. A Kissingerian strategy that eschews liberal ideology could facilitate a shift in relations.

Are concerns over deepening ties between Russia and China valid? After all, a prevalent and long-standing view in the West is that Moscow and Beijing's competing interests and close geographic proximity preclude a return to something akin to the Sino–Soviet Alliance. Nevertheless, one fact of international politics is that change is constant and assuming the way things are is the way they will always be is a poor basis for analysis in what is an increasingly dynamic international environment. At a basic level the US, Russia, and China exist in a triangular relationship: Significant shifts in bilateral relations between two can lead to a recalibration in ties – evident in the level and depth of cooperation – with the third. The shift in relations between Moscow and Beijing, and Washington and Beijing, in the early 1970s, provides one example of these dynamics; the growth in Russia–China links since 2014 provides another. It has taken place during the same period US–Russian relations deteriorated in a tit-for-tat spiral: the Maidan Revolution in 2014 swept Ukraine's pro-Russian President Viktor Yanukovych from power; Russia responded by seizing Crimea and supporting separatists in eastern Ukraine; the West then countered by imposing sanctions on Russia. Meanwhile, competition between the US and China has intensified over the same period, and especially after the Trump administration came to power in January 2017. The 2019 Worldwide Threat Assessment report by the US Office of the Director of National Intelligence confirms the interrelationship, stating that China and Russia "have significantly expanded their cooperation, especially in the energy, military, and technology spheres, *since 2014*" (Coats, 2019, 24). They are, at present, "more aligned than at any point since the mid-1950s" (Ibid.).[5]

Although a formal military Sino–Russian alliance looks unlikely owing to China's formal policy of not entering into military alliances, a number of scholars have catalogued their advancing ties (Gabuev, 2015; Cox, 2016; Malle, 2017; Gabuev, 2018; Blank, 2019) and Artyom Lukin argues that Moscow and Beijing's existing relationship represents a "quasi alliance" (Hawthorne, 2019). Furthermore, Putin has overtly referred to Sino–Russian ties as an alliance on more than one occasion to send a "message both to China and to the West" that Russia is "ready to embrace China more" (Ibid.). For his part, Chinese President Xi Jinping has called Putin his "best friend" (BBC, 2019). Expanding on this, Alexander Korolev contends that the institutional foundations for a new Sino–Russian military alliance have been established, with only "minor steps" required to cement it (Korolev, 2019).

The prospect that Chinese–Russian military and political relations will evolve to the point where they constitute, in practice if not in name, an alliance relationship in which both pledge to provide military support to one another during conflicts is no longer implausible.[6] Recent developments in Russian–Chinese links add weight to this claim. For a start, the two Eurasian giants have found ways to manage their relationship in Central Asia, the Far East, and Arctic – three regions where intense conflicts of interest were expected (Stronski and Nicole Ng, 2018; Kaczmarski, 2019; Auerswald and Anderson, 2019). In the military sphere, they have conducted joint naval drills in the Baltic and Mediterranean Seas, and engaged in multilateral military exercises with members of the Shanghai Cooperation Organization (SCO) (which includes Russia, China, Kazakhstan, Uzbekistan, Kyrgyzstan, and Tajikistan) in Central Asia (Majumdar, 2017). China has participated in military drills in Russia, including Vostock-2018 (an exercise originally designed to improve the Soviet Union's preparedness to fight China) (Carlson, 2018) and

Tsentr-2019 (Ellyatt, 2019), and in late July 2019 South Korea and Japan scrambled fighter jets to intercept the first-ever joint Chinese and Russia air patrol comprised of long-range bombers and spy planes (Osborn and Lee, 2019).

Ties are also advancing in matters of strategic nuclear deterrence. Russian President Vladimir Putin announced in October 2019 that Russia was helping China create an anti-missile early-warning system (Stefanovich, 2019). This will play a critical role in Beijing's nuclear deterrent while the secrecy surrounding this technology, and the fact it will provide Russia with insight of China's radars and early warning networks, reflects increasing levels of trust between the two (STRATFOR, 2019). Additionally, both conducted joint ballistic missile defense simulation drills in December 2017 and are united in their opposition to US ballistic missile defense programs (Steff and Khoo, 2014a, 2014b, 2017), which they claim are a threat to their deterrents and designed to provide the US with nuclear primacy (Majumdar, 2017). Chinese officers are studying at Russian military academic institutions and military–industrial technological partnerships are growing (Gady, 2019). Regarding the latter, Russia has altered its policy of not selling China its most technologically advanced military equipment and now sells China Sukhoi Su-35S fighter jets as well as its S-300 and S-400 missile defense and anti-aircraft systems (Ibid.).

Oil and gas are a centerpiece of their economic relationship, with Russia China's number one supplier of oil – a relationship cemented by the start of the Power of Siberia natural gas pipeline in December 2019 (Sassi, 2019). At the same time, bilateral trade is increasing between them and China's Belt and Road (investment) Initiatives are formally collaborating with Russia's Eurasian Economic Union (Svetlicinii, 2018). At the global level, China and Russian interests have been aligning through their rejection of liberal democratic values, America's efforts to spread those values, and aspects of the rules-based international order. They have a shared view of cyberspace where they promote the concept of 'internet sovereignty' – the idea that states have a right to limit the internet traffic and types of content that flow into and through their states – a vision that stands in sharp opposition to Western-led efforts to promote a free and open global internet. As part of this, China operates the 'Great Firewall' while Russia has successfully tested 'unplugging' its internet from the global web (Wakefield, 2019). Signaling their intention to deepen cooperation, in 2018 Moscow and Beijing pledged to "build up cooperation in all areas, and further build up strategic contacts and coordination between their armed forces, improve the existing mechanisms of military cooperation, expand interaction in the field of practical military and military–technical cooperation and jointly resist challenges to global and regional security" (Gady, 2019).

Ultimately, an entente makes a lot of sense for Moscow and Beijing. They will no longer be compelled to deploy military forces along their border to deter or defend against one another in a military contingency, freeing up those forces to place pressure, in Russia's case, on former Soviet states and eastern/central Europe to bend to its desires, and for China to expand its naval power out into the Pacific. Moreover, they both strengthen one another through sustained and growing economic, energy, and technological trade. So why, despite incentives to prevent a de facto or formal Russian–Chinese alliance from emerging, has Washington made little headway in disrupting this partnership?

US–Russia relations: The Blob strikes back

This section provides a case study of the way in which domestic bureaucratic impediments in the form of the 'Blob' – a term coined by Obama's Deputy National Security Advisor, Ben Rhodes, for the foreign policy establishment – marshaled to forestall policy change. The Blob includes intellectuals and politicians from both political parties, officials and practitioners throughout the State Department, and Washington DC's think tank community (Porter, 2018; Walt, 2018). The privileged position of these foreign policy intellectuals allows them to resist the implementation of policy ideas they find objectionable and to continually project their views through the media. Relevant to the discussion here is that liberal internationalist ideology is broadly shared across this group (even if a number of members on the Republican side would reject the label, they have their own variant of it in the form of Neoconservatism), and its collective fear is that Trump represents a threat to the established (largely liberal democratic) American security order. Patrick Porter summarizes its influence: "The Blob enjoys a number of advantages. As well as influence within the security bureaucracy, it can attack the legitimacy of measures that offend tradition. It can act through the courts and the quiet resistance of civil servants, and articulate alternatives through well-funded think tanks. It has strong institutional platforms in Congress, links to a powerful business community, and a network of nongovernmental organizations" (Porter, 2018). Hal Brands continues, "the foreign policy bureaucracy is internationalist to its core, and can be expected to use the dark arts of foot-dragging and bureaucratic warfare to resist isolationist or radical impulses" (Brands, 2017, 90). Furthermore, its influence and institutionalization are the product of years of legislative and executive decisions reacting to and shaping the international environment. As such, the Trump administration (and, it would seem, Trump specifically) has often wrestled with cabinet secretaries and agency heads in pursuit of its foreign policy agenda.[7]

The story of the failed attempt by the Trump administration to change US policy on Russia reveals the Blob's influence and highlights the kinds of tensions the administration faces as it seeks to alter US foreign policy. As a presidential nominee, Donald Trump avoided criticizing Russia's behavior on numerous occasions. Instead, he praised Russian President Vladimir Putin as a strong leader, stressed their common interests in fighting the Islamic State, and said during a Fox News interview on April 28, 2016, that "If we can make a great deal for our country and get along with Russia, that would be a tremendous thing ... I would love to try it" (Fox News, 2016).

It is worth pausing to note that Henry Kissinger, during the Obama–Trump presidential transition, apparently lobbied for closer US–Russian ties to contain China (Allen-Ebrahimian, Desiderio, Stein, and Suebsaeng, 2018). He also agreed with Trump's "general attitude" toward Russia (World Economic Forum, 2017), has met with Trump on a number of occasions (and separately with Putin), refused to join 122 members of the Republican national security community in signing a letter critiquing then-presidential candidate Trump's foreign policy positions and suitability to be president during the 2016 US presidential election (War on the Rocks, 2016),[8] and sat in the front row during the signing ceremony of the US–China Phase I trade deal (White House, 2020). Moreover, despite Trump's contempt for the judgment of America's foreign policy elite, he has expressed admiration of Kissinger, referring to him as a "friend" and "a man of immense talent, and experience, and knowledge" (White House, 2017, 2020).

Shortly after Trump was sworn into office, administration officials took steps to normalize relations with Russia. Michael Isikoff (2017) reported in the first weeks of the new administration Trump officials engaged in a bureaucratic battle with former Obama officials and State Department staffers who sought to prevent the new administration from normalizing ties. Apparently, incoming members of the Trump administration tasked State Department staffers with developing proposals to lift sanctions from Russia and return diplomatic compounds, reversing steps taken by Obama in retaliation for Russia's intervention in Ukraine and for interference in the 2016 election (Ibid.). Tom Malinowski, President Obama's Assistant Secretary of State for Human Rights, recounts that he joined in efforts to lobby Congress after former colleagues informed him the Trump administration's plan involved forging a "grand bargain" with Russia by lifting sanctions and arranging a summit between Trump and Putin (Ibid.). This played out at the same time a political scandal engulfed the president and key administration officials over their suspected ties to Russia, and concerns were voiced over potential collusion between Trump's political campaign and Russian operatives to swing the election in Trump's favor. This led to speculation he was seeking to reward Russia for assisting his electoral victory or was, himself, a Russian asset, ultimately leading to a formal investigation into ties between Trump's electoral campaign and Russia (Mueller, 2019).

To ensure Trump could not rapidly lift sanctions without Congressional approval, State Department officials rallied the Senate to codify existing sanctions against Russia imposed by earlier administrations, culminating in passage of the Countering America's Adversaries Through Sanctions Act (CAATSA) on July 27, 2017. Forced to sign the bill, Trump was critical stating it was "seriously flawed" since it reduced his ability to negotiate. He went on to note that the sanctions made "it harder for the United States to strike good deals for the American people" and "will drive China, Russia, and North Korea *much closer together*" (Trump, 2017a) – an outcome the administration sought to prevent by lifting sanctions. As a result, US–Russia relations have remained frosty throughout the Trump presidency. On one hand, the president has continued to praise Putin and disagrees with US intelligence claims that Russia interfered in the 2016 election. Moreover (against the advice of aides), Trump congratulated Putin on his re-election victory in March 2018 (BBC, 2018), has continued to suggest it is in the US interest to cooperate with Russia (Fox News, 2020), and held a summit in Helsinki with Putin in July 2018, a meeting Kissinger said "had to take place. I have advocated it for several years" (Luce, 2018). According to *The Daily Beast*, a former Trump administration official familiar with the rationale behind the summit said "It's the reverse of the Nixon–China play ... Russia and China are cozying up to each other and it is a lethal combination if they're together. China by itself is a far greater danger" (Stein, Markay and Suebsaeng, 2018).

In essence, a serious realignment of US foreign policy is anathema to members of the Blob. This group has not just lobbied the president to uphold existing arrangements but also, owing to their expertise and the administration's initial staffing shortage (which was compounded by a number of capable foreign policy bureaucrats refusing to work for the administration on principle), was able to secure a number of staffing positions throughout the administration to defend the status quo. The way this group could successfully engage in a bureaucratic battle with incoming Trump officials to resist the normalization of US–Russia relations (and encourage the codification of sanctions into law through CAATSA) is a clear example of how it can use the "dark arts of foot-dragging and bureaucratic warfare" (Brands, 2017, 90) to prevent initiatives it disagrees with.

The benefits and costs of a Kissingerian strategy

Relations with authoritarian states

The Trump administration appears to believe that enacting a Kissingerian strategy outweighs the costs of rejecting America's liberal ideology as a major element in US foreign policy. Whatever theoretical merits the strategy has, it certainly has not improved relations with Russia. With America's Middle Eastern allies, relations have been excellent since 2016. Here, Trump broke with normal protocol by making Saudi Arabia the destination of his first major foreign trip. Although the administration's policies towards Riyadh and other Middle Eastern allies have not differed markedly from Obama-era policies (the tone has differed, with Trump choosing not to chastise them for their human rights records), ending the Joint Comprehensive Plan of Action (JCPOA) with Iran and applying maximum pressure against Tehran was welcomed by US allies (Gause, 2018).

Has a Kissingerian strategy improved US relations with other not free or partly free states – such as Turkey, the Philippines, and North Korea[9] – where it could be expected to produce a positive shift? Chapter 2 provided an overview of the schizophrenic nature of US–North Korean bilateral relationship since 2016. Consistent with a Kissingerian strategy, the president has been careful to not criticize Pyongyang's human rights record or suggest that differences over values play a role in his calculus. Yet, at a macro level, Pyongyang retains its ballistic missile and nuclear weapons program – a failure of US policy, albeit one that has vexed every American administration since the end of the Cold War. On the other hand, it appears that some kind of rapport was established between Kim and Trump, and the escalating spiral of enmity was stopped in its tracks by Trump's announcement to meet with Kim in June 2018. At present, however, there are no plans for future summits and working-level talks have broken down (Atwood and Salama, 2020) and, if the objective of shifting illiberal states' ties away from Beijing applies to North Korea, the Trump administration's maximum pressure campaign has made

Pyongyang more dependent today on China than it was prior to 2016; for Pyongyang, China is its only economic lifeline (Eun-hyoung, 2019). Ultimately, the relationship is at a standstill, with potential for both an improvement and serious deterioration in US–North Korea relations.

US–Turkey rapport has soured over the latter's purchase of S-400 air defense missile systems from Russia (Macias, 2019) and increasing levels of domestic repression that have concerned the US Congress (Trump, predictably, has not criticized Ankara for the latter behavior). The S-400 purchase led the US to expel Turkey from the F-35 fighter jet program, and there is speculation that Turkey could eventually be ejected from NATO and subject to Western sanctions. It appears, however, that the administration's approach so far has prevented what would have been swifter deterioration of US–Turkey relations under other administrations, with the president requesting sanctions be delayed to create time to try to find a compromise over the S-400 issue and criticizing the Obama administration for its approach to business dealings with Turkey (Bar'el, 2019). Furthermore, Trump caused outrage across the US foreign policy community when he acquiesced by withdrawing US supports for Kurds in northern Syria and not taking stronger measures against Turkey after it invaded the area to set up a 'safe zone' for Syrian refugees, only placing sanctions on Turkish ministers (Zanotti and Thomas, 2019). Finally, during a visit by Erdoğan to the White House in November 2019, President Trump apparently arranged for a meeting between Erdoğan, Trump, and five Republican senators opposed to Turkey's purchase of S-400 systems to show Erdoğan that Trump's hands were personally tied over the issue (Klein, Diamond, Acosta, and Liptak, 2019). Despite this, the CAATSA could eventually force the president to impose sanctions on Ankara – another example of the Blob's influence.

Regarding US–Philippines affairs, there is little evidence the Trump administration has fundamentally altered the trajectory one way or another. Here Duterte's desire to hedge between the various Asia-Pacific great powers and actions by the US Senate in defense of human rights in the Philippines appear to be the chief causes leading to a deterioration of relations. For context, Philippines' President Rodrigo Duterte has sought to, even prior to the Trump administration, diversify the Philippine's foreign relations, by signing trade and infrastructure deals with China and a military cooperation agreement with Russia for example (Vicedo, 2017). Duterte even suggested a desire to "open alliances" with Russia and China, and hedged his position by sustaining close US–Philippine military ties, underpinned by the Mutual Defense Treaty and joint military exercises (Ibid.), while also threatening to terminate the 1999 Visiting Forces Agreement (VFA). On February 11, 2020, Manila gave notice to Washington that it intended to terminate the VFA within 180 days, making good on a threat to withdraw from the treaty in January 2020 in response to the US canceling the US visa for Philippine Senator Ronald dela Rosa. While no reason had been given for the visa cancellation, it was presumably because of dela Rosa's involvement in human rights violations when he enforced an anti-drug crackdown in 2016 as National Police Chief (Gomez, 2020). This takes place against the backdrop of a new budget, approved by the US Congress, containing provisions against any Philippine official found responsible for the incarceration of Senator Leila de Lima, a political opponent of Duterte (Reuters, 2019).

Relations with NATO allies

The reaction of America's NATO allies is critical to determining the costs of a Kissingerian strategy; if key US allies establish strategic autonomy or actively hard balance against American power that would constitute a major blow to America's global influence. At worst it could signal a rift in the Western world and the emergence of a new strategic competitor and pole of power in the emerging multipolar system. Here, three realist–structural forces are contributing to the Trump administration's approach to NATO. The first driver is a product of a more competitive multipolar world in which alliances are less fixed. Schweller writes, "today's friend may be tomorrow's enemy (or, at a minimum, competitor), and vice versa. Trump accepts this. He is operating according to the realpolitik principle that former US Secretary of State Henry Kissinger once summarized: 'America has no permanent friends or enemies, only interests'" (Schweller, 2018c, 141). Trump's critiques of NATO members for not pulling their weight and the European Union, which he cast as a "foe" on trade, accord with this principle (Contiguglia, 2018). The second concerns international political–economic arrangements that, in turn, connect US policy on NATO to structural forces that relate to the president's domestic objectives outlined in Chapter 1. For example, in March 2016 Trump declared, "NATO is unfair, economically, to us, to the United States. Because it really helps them more so than the United States, and we pay a disproportionate share" (Goldfarb, 2016). At other times, he stated, "NATO was set up a long time ago – many, many years ago when things were different ... We were a rich nation then. We had nothing but money. We had nothing but power," "NATO is costing us a fortune", and the US must be "properly reimbursed" for protecting Europe (Bandow, 2016; Sloan, 2018, 5). This occurs despite the fact that

Europe has a similar GDP to the US and a larger population (Friedman, 2017). Barry Posen sums up the point by declaring it amounts to "welfare for the rich" – effectively a transfer of funds from the US to Europe (Posen, 2016). This 'subsidization' is a state of affairs that allows NATO's European members to direct funds away from defense to social welfare and domestic industries, all of which comes at the expense of American industries and working-class jobs that Trump has promised his domestic constituents he will restore. Friedman outlines a third cause, asserting that: "Trump's core strategic argument is that the United States is overextended ... Washington is entangled in complex relationships that place risks and burdens on the United States to come to the aid of some countries. However, its commitments are not matched by those countries in capability, nor in intent" (Friedman, 2017). In this view, Washington's NATO allies do not commensurately reciprocate with regard to US strategic interests, which since 2001 have existed outside of Europe in Afghanistan and Iraq, and now extends to China. These efforts have cost the US immensely in terms of blood and treasure – approximately \$5.9trn according to one study (Crawford 2018) – accelerating the transition of the international system from unipolarity to multipolarity. Friedman explains that in these conflicts America's NATO allies have "not provided decisive strategic support", and been "far below the abilities of NATO members" (Friedman, 2017). In this view Washington's NATO allies have not contributed enough to America's strategic priorities, leaving the US to bear the brunt of the cost of recent wars in the Middle East, further reducing US national strength and structural power. Thus, "It is therefore not clear that NATO as currently constituted is of value to the United States" (Ibid.), and altering US–NATO relations is a logical response.

How have America's European NATO allies reacted? They appear to be edging towards a posture of greater strategic independence. At worst, a scenario that seemed all but inconceivable only a few years ago would emerge whereby Europeans actively hard balance against the US. Consider, in May 2018, Germany's Chancellor, Angela Merkel, said "It's no longer the case that the United States will simply just protect us"; French President Emmanuel Macron called for, in November 2018, "a true European army ... to protect ourselves with respect to China, Russia and *even the United States of America*"; and European Commission President Ursula von der Leyen said in January 2020 that Europe needed "credible military capabilities" (Sharkov, 2018; Stone 2018; Brown and Herszenhorn, 2020). Alongside this, there has been lobbying to strengthen the Common Security and Defense Policy, while a slew of new defense initiatives have been created such as the European Defense Fund, Permanent Structured Cooperation, and

Coordinated Annual Review (Brattberg and Valasek, 2019). It is impossible to know how far these efforts will go. After all, balancing occurs in degrees (Levy, 2002, 134) and the aforementioned statements suggest European leaders are in a pre-balancing phase. While active or hard balancing (for a discussion on the types of balancing see Steff and Khoo, 2014b, 224–227) against US power may never eventuate, European concern over the US role in the world is real and greater strides towards strategic autonomy are likely. However, it is also possible that this is just a hedge should Trump's rhetoric be turned into reality and the US start significantly reducing its commitment to European defense. There is no sign of this at the moment as a number of official documents, like the 2017 NSS, note that "a strong and free Europe is of vital importance to the United States" (White House, 2017, 47). Furthermore, the US continues to join NATO military exercises; US defense expenditure in Europe actually increased in 2018 (including stationing additional forces in Poland); and the administration has re-iterated its support for Ukraine's independence – a bellwether issue as some European states would view a decline in US support for Ukraine against Russia as a sign the US was preparing to downgrade its support for NATO as a whole and preparing to reach a grand bargain with Moscow at the expense of European security. In any event, the Europeans will likely incrementally deepen their military integration while hoping that Trump's successor strongly reasserts America's commitment to European defense in rhetoric and practice.

Conclusion

Power across the international system is likely to continue to diffuse away from the US in coming years, with a multipolar configuration generating a greater level of competition between the most powerful nations. In the emergent multipolar system, the Trump administration has responded to systemic pressures by downplaying the role ideology should perform in foreign policy, renouncing the goal of promoting liberal democracy and values, and/or engaging in nation-building abroad, as these efforts could leave Washington at a disadvantage in its competition with China. In short, ideological impulses reduce the flexibility of US foreign policy and, at a time of American decline, discipline is required to return the US to narrow conceptions of the national interest; ideology is an indulgence.

Applying a structural frame to the analysis of the Trump administration's foreign policy suggests there are reasons beyond President Trump's personal distaste of America's liberal allies that could motivate his verbal attacks against them – it further communicates the point to illiberal states that the Trump administration does not require regimes to be liberal to receive friendship and support. If illiberal states believe the US poses little threat to their regimes – a perception theoretically strengthened by downplaying liberalism – it could increase their incentives to lean towards the United States. This has hallmarks of the Nixon–Kissinger strategy that prevailed in the 1970s. In this context, the chapter examined the triangle of US–Russian–China interactions where pressures exist for the US to improve relations with Russia to undermine a budding Sino–Russia alliance, efforts disrupted by the Blob. If an anti-China coalition of mixed liberal and authoritarian regimes is necessary to check China's global ambitions, the Blob may very well constitute the most significant force that prevents its emergence. The consequence of the codification of sanctions against Russia has been a deterioration in US–Russian relations during the Trump presidency – here the ties (real or imagined) with Trump and some of his close aides, and Russia's interference in the 2016 election, have complicated efforts to improve relations by generating domestic resistance. This shows how domestic political factors can impede adjustments designed to respond to structural challenges.

Beyond the failed attempt to improve US–Russian ties, the chapter also considered whether a Kissingerian strategy delivered benefits in relation to a number of not free and partly free authoritarian states. It found that, at the margins, it may have made a difference to US relations with some, but has made little headway with others. US–NATO links are a point of concern. Here, even though the administration's policy has not radically changed – the US remains militarily committed to Europe's defense – Trump's verbal attacks against America's NATO allies have led some officials to increase their lobbying for Europe to shift on to a more independent footing, leading to some new defense initiatives. The first stages of balancing or a shift towards strategic autonomy from Washington is underway, although it is by no means certain that it will turn into something substantive.

Finally, it's likely the president's inflammatory rhetoric and renunciation of support for democratic and human rights abroad has contributed to a decline in America's global standing since 2015 (Pew Research Center, 2020). Has this redounded in China's favor? Has Washington lost an edge, ideologically, in its competition for the hearts and minds of foreign populations and leaders? There is no direct evidence showing that China's ties have significantly improved with states because of this although it may have contributed to its lobbying efforts to get countries to sign up to the Asian Infrastructure Bank, Belt and Road Initiatives, and accept Chinese companies building out their 5G networks. China is also facing its own public standing headwinds due to revelations over its 'education camps' in Xinjiang, ongoing protests in Hong Kong, and growing concerns over growing authoritarian trends at home – factors that may restrain some foreign leaders from moving nearer to Beijing.

Ultimately, the president is responding to structural forces in ways particular to his personality; there is nothing about the structure that dictates the methods through which he is seeking to pursue a Kissingerian strategy. In fact, it appears his verbal critiques of US allies and international institutions have generated consternation among the Washington foreign policy bureaucracy that is tasked with delivering US policy. In turn, this has significantly impeded the ability of the Trump administration to forge a significantly more flexible global posture.

The next and concluding chapter returns to the question of how individual, domestic, and international forces interact to produce the foreign policy outcomes considered throughout this book. It then considers the implications of Trump's foreign policy tactics and strategy for the future of interstate relations.

Notes

1 Word limits do not allow a full recounting of how structural forces influenced the Obama administration's foreign policy but it is notable that, like the Trump administration, it sought to elevate realist principles in foreign policy and place greater constraints on the use of American power abroad. For a small selection of the literature on Obama's foreign policy see Stepak and Whitlark (2012), Goldberg (2016), Kaufman (2016), Bentley and Holland (2017), and Clarke and Ricketts (2017).
2 For a catalogue of the ways Trump showed his contempt for the US's liberal allies, norms and values, see Brands (2017, 17) and Powaski (2019).
3 The G7 consists of the world's seven largest advanced economies (Canada, France, Germany, Italy, Japan, Britain, and the United States).
4 Trump commended Duterte for conducting a campaign of extrajudicial executions against drug dealers; congratulated Erdoğan for winning an election victory in April 2017 that was widely viewed as rigged; has not criticized China's 're-education' camps in Xinjiang; and not critiqued the killing of journalists in Russia.
5 Even think tanks that are critical of Russia's behavior are mindful of growing Sino–Russian ties. In *Rising to the China Challenge*, authors affiliated with the Center for a New American Century who served in the Bush, Obama, and Trump administrations, recommend exemptions be made for countries such as India, Indonesia, and Vietnam to purchase Russian weapons if they are doing so to balance China. While the report says the US "should seek to reduce Russian revenue from overseas arms sales" by providing affordable options for states to purchase US weaponry over the long term, it also notes "further isolating Russia in Asia and preventing its arms sales to a variety of states could push Moscow into a closer and more co-dependent relationship with Beijing" (Ratner et al., 2020).

6 The basis for this exists in Article 9 of the 2001 bilateral Treaty of Good Neighborliness and Friendly Cooperation between the People's Republic of China and the Russian Federation. It declares "when a situation arises in which one of the contracting parties deems that peace is being threatened and undermined or its security interests are involved or when it is confronted with the threat of aggression, the contracting parties shall immediately hold contacts and consultations in order to eliminate such threats" (Ministry of Foreign Affairs of the People's Republic of China, 2001).

7 By way of basic illustration was the president's desire to remove US forces from Syria and Afghanistan and the pushback from the Pentagon. The *Washington Post,* in reporting on the resignation of then Secretary of Defense James Mattis in December 2018, claimed that the president's desire to withdraw US forces from Syria and Afghanistan stood out as causes for the resignation (Sonne et al., 2018). This story highlights both the kinds of tensions the administration faces as it seeks to alter US foreign policy as well as the way in which the machinery can impede it.

8 During an interview on CBS, Kissinger said "Donald Trump is a phenomenon that foreign countries haven't seen… So it is a shocking experience to them that he came into office, at the same time, extraordinary opportunity. And I believe he has the possibility of going down in history as a very considerable president… a new president who is asking a lot of unfamiliar questions" (CBS News, 2016).

9 According to *Freedom House*'s country rankings, Turkey and North Korea are coded 'not free' and the Philippines 'partly free'. While US relations with many other countries could be considered, word limits have restricted me from considering additional ones.

Bibliography

Allen-Ebrahimian, Bethany, Andrew Desiderio, Sam Stein, and Asawin Suebsaeng. Henry Kissinger Pushed Trump to Work with Russia to Box in China. July 31, 2018. *The Daily Beast.* Retrieved from https://www.thedailybeast.com/henry-kissinger-pushed-trump-to-work-with-russia-to-box-in-china.

Allison, Graham. The New Spheres of Influence: Sharing the Globe with Other Great Powers. 2020. *Foreign Affairs*, 99(30): 30–40.

Arms Control Association. Chronology of U.S.–North Korean Nuclear and Missile Diplomacy. July 2019. Retrieved from https://www.armscontrol.org/factsheets/dprkchron.

Atwood, Kylie, and Vivian Salama. Trump Tells Advisers He Doesn't Want Another Summit with North Korea's Kim before the Election. February 10, 2020. *CNN.* Retrieved from https://edition.cnn.com/2020/02/10/politics/trump-north-korea-thaw/index.html.

Auerswald, David, and Terry L. Anderson. China, Russia Move into the Arctic – and Put US at Risk. May 14, 2019. *The Hill.* Retrieved from https://thehill.com/opinion/national-security/443324-china-russia-move-into-the-arctic-and-put-us-at-risk.

Bandow, Doug. Donald Trump Asks: Why Should America Defend Europeans Who Won't Defend Themselves? August 1, 2016. *Forbes*. Retrieved from https://www.forbes.com/sites/dougbandow/2016/08/01/donald-trump-asks-why-should-america-defend-europeans-who-wont-defend-themselves/#b7066f071aba.

Bar'el, Zvi. With His Good Pal Trump in the White House, Erdogan's Conquests Will Be Much Easier, July 5, 2019. *Haaretz*. Retrieved from https://www.haaretz.com/middle-east-news/.premium-with-his-good-pal-trump-in-the-white-house-erdogan-s-conquests-will-be-much-easier-1.7450520.

Barbash, Fred. Bush: Iraq Part of 'Global Democratic Revolution'. November 6, 2003. *The Washington Post*. Retrieved from www.washingtonpost.com/wp-dyn/articles/A7991-2003Nov6.html.

BBC. Trump 'Warned' Not to Congratulate Putin in Russia Election. March 21, 2018. Retrieved from https://www.bbc.com/news/world-us-canada-43488358.

BBC. G7 Summit Ends in Disarray as Trump Abandons Joint Statement. June 10, 2018. Retrieved from https://www.bbc.com/news/world-us-canada-44427660.

BBC. China's Xi Praises 'Best Friend' Putin during Russia Visit. June 6, 2019. Retrieved from https://www.bbc.com/news/world-europe-48537663.

Bentley, Michelle, and Jack Holland. *The Obama Doctrine: A Legacy of Continuity in US Foreign Policy?* London: Routledge, 2016.

Blank, Stephen. The Russo-Chinese Alliance: What Are Its Limits? (An Emerging China–Russia Axis? Implications for the United States in an Era of Strategic Competition). Testimony before the U.S. China Economic and Security Review Commission Session. March 21, 2019. Retrieved from https://www.uscc.gov/sites/default/files/Blank_Testimony.pdf.

Brands, Hal. *What Good is Grand Strategy? Power and Purpose in American Statecraft from Harry S. Truman to George W. Bush*. Ithaca, NY: Cornell University Press, 2014.

Brands, Hal. The Unexceptional Superpower: American Grand Strategy in the Age of Trump. 2017. *Survival*, 59(6): 7–40.

Brands, Hal. *American Grand Strategy in the Age of Trump*. Washington, DC: Brookings Institution Press, 2018.

Brattberg, Erik, and Tomas Valasek. EU Defense Cooperation: Progress amid Transatlantic Concerns. November 21, 2019. *Carnegie Endowment*. Retrieved from https://carnegieendowment.org/2019/11/21/eu-defense-cooperation-progress-amid-transatlantic-concerns-pub-80381.

Brooks, Stephen, and William Wohlforth. The Rise and Fall of the Great Powers in the Twenty-first Century: China's Rise and the Fate of America's Global Position. 2015/2016. *International Security*, 40(3): 7–53.

Brown Stephen, and David M. Herszenhorn. Von der Leyen: EU Must Develop 'Credible Military Capabilities'. January 22, 2020. *Politico*. Retrieved from https://www.politico.eu/article/ursula-von-der-leyen-eu-military-capabilities/.

Bush, George W. *Decision Points*. New York: Crown Publishers, 2010.

Carlson, Brian. Vostok-2018: Another Sign of Strengthening Russia–China Ties. November 2018. *SWP-Berlin*. Retrieved from https://www.swp-berlin. org/en/publication/vostok-2018-another-sign-of-strengthening-russia-china-ties/.

CBS News. Face the Nation Transcript: Conway, Kissinger, Donilon. December 18, 2016. Retrieved from https://www.cbsnews.com/news/face-the-nation-transcript-conway-kissinger-donilon/.

Cha, Taesuh, and Jungkun Seo. Trump by Nixon: Maverick Presidents in the Years of U.S. Relative Decline. 2018. *Korean Journal of Defense Analysis*, 30(1): 79–96.

Clark, Gen. Wesley K. *Winning Modern Wars: Iraq Terrorism, and the American Empire*. New York: Public Affairs, 2003.

Clarke, Michael. The Belt and Road Initiative: China's New Grand Strategy? 2017. *Asia Policy*, 24: 71–79.

Clarke, Michael, and Anthony Ricketts. Did Obama Have a Grand Strategy? 2017. *Journal of Strategic Studies*, 40(1–2): 295–324.

CNN. You are Either with Us or Against Us. November 6, 2001. Retrieved from https://edition.cnn.com/2001/US/11/06/gen.attack.on.terror/

Coats, Daniel R. Worldwide Threat Assessment of the US Intelligence Community, Senate Select Committee on Intelligence. January 29, 2019. Retrieved from https://www.dni.gov/files/ODNI/documents/2019-ATA-SFR---SSCI.pdf.

Contiguglia, Cat. Trump: EU is One of United States' Biggest Foes. July 15, 2018. *Politico*. Retrieved from https://www.politico.eu/article/donald-trump-putin-russia-europe-one-of-united-states-biggest-foes/.

Cox, Michael. Not Just 'Convenient': China and Russia's New Strategic Partnership in the Age of Geopolitics. December 2016. *Asian Journal of Comparative Politics*, 1(4): 317–334.

Crawford, Neta C. $5.9 Trillion Spent and Obligated on Post-9/11 Wars. November 16, 2018. Watson Institute. Retrieved from https://watson.brown. edu/research/2018/59-trillion-spent-and-obligated-post-911-wars.

Department of Defense. 2018 National Defense Strategy of the United States. 2018. Retrieved from https://dod.defense.gov/Portals/1/Documents/pubs/2018-National-Defense-Strategy-Summary.pdf.

Desch, Michael. America's Liberal Illiberalism: The Ideological Origins of Overreaction in U.S. Foreign Policy. Winter 2007/2008. *International Security*, 32(2): 7–43.

Ellyatt, Holly. Russia Conducts Massive Military Drills with China, Sending a Message to the West. September 17, 2019. *CNBC*. Retrieved from https:// www.cnbc.com/2019/09/17/russia-conducts-tsentr-2019-military-exercises-with-china-and-india.html.

Eun-hyoung, Kim. N. Korea's Trade Dependence on China Has Increased to 90% over Last 3 Years. December 2, 2019. *Hankyoreh*. Retrieved from http://english.hani.co.kr/arti/english_edition/e_northkorea/919283.html.

European Parliament. Closer to the Citizens, Closer to the Ballot. Spring 2019. Retrieved from https://www.europarl.europa.eu/at-your-service/files/be-heard/eurobarometer/2019/closer-to-the-citizens-closer-to-the-ballot/report/en-eurobarometer-2019.pdf.

Fox News. Donald Trump on his Foreign Policy Strategy. April 29, 2016. Retrieved from www.foxnews.com/transcript/2016/04/29/donald-trump-on-his-foreign-policy-strategy.html.

Fox News. Interview: Laura Ingraham Interviews Donald Trump on Fox's the Ingraham Angle. January 10, 2020. Retrieved from https://factba.se/transcript/donald-trump-interview-laura-ingraham-fox-news-january-10-2020.

Freedom House. *Democracy in Crisis*. 2018. Retrieved from https://freedomhouse.org/report/freedom-world/freedom-world-2018.

Freedom House. *Democracy in Retreat*. 2019. Retrieved from https://freedomhouse.org/report/freedom-world/freedom-world-2019.

Friedberg, Aaron L. Competing with China. 2018. *Survival*, 60(3): 7–64.

Friedman, George. Donald Trump Has a Coherent, Radical Foreign Policy Doctrine. January 20, 2017. *RealClearWorld*. Retrieved from https://www.realclearworld.com/articles/2017/01/20/donald_trump_has_a_coherent_radical_foreign_policy_doctrine_112180.html.

Friedman, Thomas L. U.S. Vision of Foreign Policy Reversed. September 22, 1993. *New York Times*. Retrieved from https://www.nytimes.com/1993/09/22/world/us-vision-of-foreign-policy-reversed.html.

Gabuev, Alexander. A 'Soft Alliance'? Russia–China Relations after the Ukraine Crisis. 2015. *European Council on Foreign Relations*. Retrieved from http://lea.vitis.uspnet.usp.br/arquivos/a-softalliance-russia-china-relations-after-the-ukraine-crisis_alexander-gabuev.pdf.

Gabuev, Alexander. Why Russia and China Are Strengthening Security Ties: Is the U.S. Driving Them Closer Together? September 24, 2018. *Foreign Affairs*. Retrieved from https://www.foreignaffairs.com/articles/china/2018-09-24/why-russia-and-china-are-strengthening-security-ties.

Gady, Franz-Stefan. Why the West Should Not Underestimate China–Russia Military Ties. January 30, 2019. *East West Institute*. Retrieved from https://www.eastwest.ngo/idea/why-west-should-not-underestimate-china-russia-military-ties.

Gause III, F. Gregory. Donald Trump and the Middle East. In (eds.) Jervis, Robert, et al. *Chaos in the Liberal Order: The Trump Presidency and International Politics in the Twenty-first Century*. New York: Columbia University Press, 2018.

Givens, John Wagner. The Beijing Consensus Is Neither: China as a Non-Ideological Challenge to International Norms. 2011. *St Antony's International Review*, 6(2): 10–26.

Goldfarb, Michael. Donald Trump and Barack Obama Agree: America Cannot Police the World Anymore. *The Telegraph*. March 30, 2016. Retrieved from https://www.telegraph.co.uk/news/2016/03/30/donald-trump-and-barack-obama-agree-america-cannot-police-the-wo/.

Goldberg, Jeffrey. The Obama Doctrine. April 2016. *The Atlantic*. Retrieved from https://www.theatlantic.com/magazine/archive/2016/04/the-obama-doctrine/471525/.

Gomez, Jim. Philippines Notifies US of Intent to End Major Security Pact. February 11, 2020. *AP News*. Retrieved from https://apnews.com/969de0066e93fbc26a4e258b7b7eca1d?fbclid=IwAR3Sv8ulkKTcH_z8aX07O-Ib0IGZIlXtoAWYNCBtLPoj7bWaBklAwYpZETc.

Graaff, Nana De, and Bastiaan Van Apeldoorn. US–China relations and the Liberal World Order: Contending Elites, Colliding Visions? 2018. *International Affairs*, 94(1): 113–131.

Hawthorne, Emily. Taking the Measure of a Russian–Chinese Alliance. November 15, 2019. *STRATFOR*. Retrieved from https://worldview.stratfor.com/article/taking-measure-russian-chinese-alliance-great-power-competition.

Hochman, Dafna. Rehabilitating a Rogue: Libya's WMD Reversal and Lessons for U.S. Policy. Spring 2006. *Parameters*, 36(1): 63–78.

Horton, Chris. China Seeks to Flip Nations in Pacific Great Game with US. August 20, 2019. *Nikkei Asian Review*. Retrieved from https://asia.nikkei.com/Spotlight/Asia-Insight/China-seeks-to-flip-nations-in-Pacific-Great-Game-with-US.

IMF. Projected GDP Ranking (2019–2024). November 12, 2019. *Statistics Times*. Retrieved from http://statisticstimes.com/economy/projected-world-gdp-ranking.php.

Isikoff, Michael. How the Trump Administration's Secret Efforts to Ease Russia Sanctions Fell Short. June 1, 2017. *Yahoo News*. Retrieved from https://news.yahoo.com/trump-administrations-secret-efforts-ease-russia-sanctions-fell-short-231301145.html.

Jackson, Van. Power, Trust, and Network Complexity: Three Logics of Hedging in Asian Security. 2014. *International Relations of the Asia-Pacific*, 14(3): 331–356.

Jentleson, Bruce W., and Christopher A. Whytock. Who "Won" Libya? The Force-Diplomacy Debate and Its Implications for Theory and Policy. Winter 2005/2006. *International Security*, 30(3): 47–86.

Jervis, Robert. Understanding the Bush Doctrine. 2003. *Political Science Quarterly*, 118(3): 365–388.

Jervis, Robert. Unipolarity: A Structural Perspective. 2009. *World Politics*, 61(1): 188–213.

Jervis, Robert. Do Leaders Matter and How Would We Know? 2013. *Security Studies*, 22(2): 153–179.

Johnson, James. *The US–China Military and Defense Relationship during the Obama Presidency*. Cham, Switzerland: Palgrave, 2018.

Kaczmarski, Marcin. Russia–China Relations in Central Asia: Why Is There a Surprising Absence of Rivalry? August 19, 2019. *Asan Forum*. Retrieved from www.theasanforum.org/russia-china-relations-in-central-asia-why-is-there-a-surprising-absence-of-rivalry/.

Kaplan, Robert. A New Cold War Has Begun. January 7, 2019. *Foreign Policy*. Retrieved from https://foreignpolicy.com/2019/01/07/a-new-cold-war-has-begun/.

Kaufman, Robert Gordon. *Dangerous Doctrine: How Obama's Grand Strategy Weakened America*. Lexington: University Press of Kentucky, 2016.

Klein, Betsy, Jeremy Diamond, Jim Acosta, and Kevin Liptak. Erdoğan Showed GOP Senators 'Surreal' Propaganda Video during WH Meeting. November 14, 2019. *CNN*. Retrieved from https://edition.cnn.com/2019/11/14/politics/trump-gop-senators-erdogan/index.html.

Kogan, Eugene B. Art of the Power Deal: The Four Negotiation Roles of Donald J. Trump. 2019. *Negotiation Journal*, 35(1): 65–83.

Korolev, Alexander. On the Verge of an Alliance: Contemporary China–Russia Military Cooperation. 2019. *Asian Security*, 15(3): 233–252.

Kuisong, Yang. The Sino–Soviet Border Clash of 1969: From Zhenbao Island to Sino–American Rapprochement. 2000. *Cold War History*, 1(1): 21–52.

Layne, Christopher. The US–Chinese Power Shift and the End of the Pax Americana. 2018. *International Affairs*, 94(1): 89–111.

Leverett, Flynn L. Why Libya Gave Up on the Bomb. January 23, 2007. *Brookings Institution*. Retrieved from www.brookings.edu/opinions/2004/0123middleeast_leverett.aspx.

Levy, Jack S. Balances and Balancing: Concepts, Propositions, and Research Design. In (eds.) John A. Vasquez and Colin Elman. *Realism and the Balancing of Power: A New Debate*. Englewood Cliffs, NJ: Prentice-Hall, 2002.

Lind, Jennifer. Life in China's Asia: What Regional Hegemony Would Look Like. 2018. *Foreign Affairs*, 97(2): 71–82.

Luce, Edward. Henry Kissinger: 'We Are in a Very Grave Period'. July 20, 2018. *Financial Times*. Retrieved from https://www.ft.com/content/926a66b0-8b49-11e8-bf9e-8771d5404543?segmentId=7ac5b61e-8d73-f906-98c6-68ac3b9ee271.

Macias, Amanda. Turkey's Multibillion-Dollar Arms Deal with Russia Casts a Shadow over NATO Summit. December 2, 2019. CNBC. Retrieved from https://www.cnbc.com/2019/12/02/turkeys-arms-deal-with-russia-casts-shadow-over-nato-summit.html.

Majumdar, Dave. Russia and China Are Doing Joint Air Defense Drills to Prepare for a Surprise Attack, December 11, 2017. *The National Interest*. Retrieved from https://nationalinterest.org/blog/the-buzz/russia-china-are-doing-joint-air-defense-drills-prepare-23611.

Malle, Silvana. Russia and China in the 21st Century. Moving Towards Cooperative Behaviour. 2017. *Journal of Eurasian Studies*, 8(2): 136–150.

Mazarr, Michael J., Timothy R. Heath, and Astrid Stuth Cevallos. China and the International Order. 2018. *RAND*. Retrieved from https://www.rand.org/content/dam/rand/pubs/research_reports/RR2400/RR2423/RAND_RR2423.pdf.

Mearsheimer, John J. Back to the Future: Instability in Europe after the Cold War. Summer 1990. *International Security*, 15(1): 5–56.

Mearsheimer, John J. Donald Trump Should Embrace a Realist Foreign Policy. November 27, 2016. *The National Interest.* Retrieved from https://nationalinterest.org/feature/donald-trump-should-embrace-realist-foreign-policy-18502.

Mearsheimer, John J. *Great Delusion: Liberal Dreams and International Realities.* New Haven, CT: Yale University Press, 2018.

Mearsheimer, John J. Bound to Fail: The Rise and Fall of the Liberal International Order. 2019. *International Security*, 43(4): 7–50.

Miller, Benjamin. Explaining Changes in U.S. Grand Strategy: 9/11, the Rise of Offensive Liberalism, and the War in Iraq. 2010. *Security Studies*, 19(1): 26–65.

Ministry of Foreign Affairs of the People's Republic of China. China–Russia Treaty. 2001. Retrieved from https://www.fmprc.gov.cn/mfa_eng/wjdt_665385/2649_665393/t15771.shtml.

Mueller, Robert S. US Department of Justice, Report on the Investigation into Russian Interference in the 2016 Presidential Election. March 2019. U.S. Department of Justice. Retrieved from https://www.justice.gov/storage/report.pdf.

NATO. Defence Expenditure of NATO Countries (2013–2019). November 29, 2019. Retrieved from https://www.nato.int/nato_static_fl2014/assets/pdf/pdf_2019_11/20191129_pr-2019-123-en.pdf.

O'Rourke, Ronald. China Naval Modernization: Implications for U.S. Navy Capabilities—Background and Issues for Congress. January 22, 2020. *Congressional Research Service.* Retrieved from https://fas.org/sgp/crs/row/RL33153.pdf.

Osborn, Andrew, and Joyce Lee. First Russian–Chinese Air Patrol in Asia-Pacific Draws Shots from South Korea. July 23, 2019. *Reuters.* Retrieved from https://www.reuters.com/article/us-southkorea-russia-aircraft/first-russian-chinese-air-patrol-in-asia-pacific-draws-shots-from-south-korea-idUSKCN1UI072.

Pew Research Center. Global Indicators Database. 2020. Retrieved from https://www.pewresearch.org/global/database/.

Pompeo, Mike. Remarks by Secretary Pompeo at the German Marshall Fund. December 4, 2018. U.S. Embassy in Ukraine. Retrieved from https://ua.usembassy.gov/remarks-by-secretary-pompeo-at-the-german-marshall-fund/.

Pompeo, Mike (a). A Foreign Policy from the Founding. May 11, 2019. *Claremont Institute.* Retrieved from https://americanmind.org/essays/a-foreign-policy-from-the-founding/.

Pompeo, Mike (b). Speech of Secretary of State Michael R. Pompeo: The China Challenge. October 30, 2019. *U.S. Embassy in Paraguay.* Retrieved from https://py.usembassy.gov/speech-of-secretary-of-state-michael-r-pompeo-the-china-challenge/.

Porter, Patrick. Why America's Grand Strategy Has Not Changed. Power, Habit, and the U.S. Foreign Policy Establishment. Spring 2018. *International Security*, 42(4): 9–46.

Posen, Barry. The High Costs and Limited Benefits of America's Alliances. August 7, 2016. *The National Interest*. Retrieved from https://nationalinterest. org/blog/the-skeptics/the-high-costs-limited-benefits-americas-alliances-17273.

Powaski, Ronald E. *Ideals, Interests, and U.S. Foreign Policy from George H.W. Bush to Donald Trump*. Ashland, OH: Palgrave Macmillan, 2019.

Ratner, Ely, and Daniel Kliman, Susanna V. Blume, Rush Doshi, Chris Dougherty, Richard Fontaine, et al. Rising to the China Challenge, Renewing American Competitiveness in the Indo-Pacific, January 28, 2020. *Center for a New American Century*. Retrieved from https://www.cnas.org/publications/ reports/rising-to-the-china-challenge.

Reuters. Philippines Bans Two U.S. Senators, Mulls New Visa Rules for Americans. December 27, 2019. *Reuters*. Retrieved from https://www. reuters.com/article/us-philippines-usa-duterte/philippines-bans-two-u-s-senators-mulls-new-visa-rules-for-americans-idUSKBN1YV0GX.

Rolland, Nadege. China's Vision for a New World Order, January 27, 2020. *NBR*. Retrieved from https://www.nbr.org/publication/chinas-vision-for-a-new-world-order/.

Ruonan, Liu, and Liu Fend. Contending Ideas on China's Non-Alliance Strategy. 2017. *Chinese Journal of International Politics*, 10(2): 151–171.

Russett, Bruce. *Grasping the Democratic Peace*. Princeton, NJ: Princeton University Press, 1993.

Sassi, Francesco. What the 'Power of Siberia' Tells us about China–Russia Relations. December 7, 2019. *The Diplomat*. Retrieved from https:// thediplomat.com/2019/12/what-the-power-of-siberia-tells-us-about-china-russia-relations/.

Schweller, Randall (a). Opposite but Compatible Nationalisms: A Neoclassical Realist Approach to the Future of US–China Relations. Spring 2018. *Chinese Journal of International Politics*, 11(1): 23–48.

Schweller, Randall L. (b). Why Trump Now: A Third–Image Explanation. In (eds.) Jervis, Robert, et al. *Chaos in the Liberal Order: The Trump Presidency and International Politics in the Twenty-First Century*. New York: Columbia University Press, 2018.

Schweller, Randall (c). Three Cheers for Trump's Foreign Policy. What the Establishment Misses. September/October 2018. *Foreign Affairs*, 97(5): 133–143.

Sharkov, Damien. Angela Merkel: Europe Can No Longer Rely on U.S. Protection. May 10, 2018. *Newsweek*. Retrieved from https://www.newsweek. com/europe-cannot-fully-rely-us-protection-anymore-says-germanys-merkel-919410.

SIPRI. Trends in World Military Expenditure 2018. April 2019. Retrieved from https://www.sipri.org/publications/2019/sipri-fact-sheets/trends-world-military-expenditure-2018.

Sloan, Stanley. Donald Trump and NATO: Historic Alliance Meets A-history President. In (ed.) Jervis, Robert, et al. *Chaos in the Liberal Order: The Trump Presidency and International Politics in the Twenty-first Century*. New York: Columbia University Press, 2018.

Sonne, Paul, Josh Dawsey, and Missy Ryan. Mattis Resigns after Clash with Trump over Troop Withdrawal from Syria and Afghanistan. December 20, 2018. *The Washington Post.* Retrieved from https://www.washingtonpost.com/world/national-security/trump-announces-mattis-will-leave-as-defense-secretary-at-the-end-of-february/2018/12/20/e1a846ee-e147-11e8-ab2c-b31dcd53ca6b_story.html.

Stefanovich, Dmitry. Russia to Help China Develop an Early Warning System. October 25, 2019. *The Diplomat.* Retrieved from https://thediplomat.com/2019/10/russia-to-help-china-develop-an-early-warning-system/.

Steff, Reuben. The Naked and the Unnerving: A Trumpian Foreign Policy. August 15, 2018. *The Globe Post.* Retrieved from https://theglobepost.com/2018/08/15/trump-foreign-policy/.

Steff, Reuben, and Nicholas Khoo (a). 'This Program Will Not Be a Threat to Them': Ballistic Missile Defense and US Relations with Russia and China. 2014. *Defense & Security Analysis*, 30(1): 17–28.

Steff, Reuben, and Nicholas Khoo (b). Hard Balancing in the Age of American Unipolarity: The Russian Response to US Ballistic Missile Defense during the Bush Administration (2001–2008). 2014. *Journal of Strategic Studies*, 37(2): 222–258.

Steff, Reuben, and Nicholas Khoo. *Security at a Price: The International Politics of US Ballistic Missile Defense.* Lanham, MD: Rowman & Littlefield, 2017.

Stein, Sam, Lachlan Markay, and Asawin Suebsaeng. Trump's Own Team: He 'Looked Incredibly Weak' Next to Putin. July 16, 2018. *The Daily Beast.* Retrieved from https://www.thedailybeast.com/trumps-own-team-he-looked-incredibly-weak-next-to-putin.

Stepak, Amir, and Rachel Whitlark. The Battle over America's Foreign Policy Doctrine. 2012. *Survival*, 54(5): 45–66.

Stone, Jon. Emmanuel Macron Calls for Creation of a 'True European Army' to Defend against Russia and the US. November 6, 2018. *The Independent.* Retrieved from https://www.independent.co.uk/news/world/europe/emmanuel-macron-european-army-france-russia-us-military-defence-eu-a8619721.html.

STRATFOR. Russia, China: Cooperation on a Missile Warning System Points to an Increasing Alignment. October 4, 2019. Retrieved from https://worldview.stratfor.com/article/russia-china-cooperation-missile-warning-system-points-increasing-alignment-great-power-competition.

Stronski, Paul, and Nicole Ng. Cooperation and Competition: Russia and China in Central Asia, the Russian Far East, and the Arctic. February 28, 2018. Retrieved from https://carnegieendowment.org/2018/02/28/cooperation-and-competition-russia-and-china-in-central-asia-russian-far-east-and-arctic-pub-75673.

Svetlicinii, Alexandr. China's Belt and Road Initiative and the Eurasian Economic Union: 'Integrating the Integrations'. March 2018. *Public Administration Issues*, 5: 7–20.

Time. Read Donald Trump's Speech on Trade. June 28, 2016. Retrieved from http://time.com/4386335/donald-trump-trade-speech-transcript/.

Trump, Donald. Full transcript: Donald Trump's Jobs Plan Speech. June 28, 2016. *Politico.* https://www.politico.com/story/2016/06/full-transcript-trump-job-plan-speech-224891.

Trump, Donald (a). Statement by President Donald J. Trump on Signing the 'Countering America's Adversaries through Sanctions Act'. August 2, 2017. Retrieved from https://www.whitehouse.gov/briefings-statements/statement-president-donald-j-trump-signing-countering-americas-adversaries-sanctions-act/.

Trump, Donald (b). Full text: Trump's 2017 U.N. speech transcript. September 19, 2017. *Politico.* https://www.politico.com/story/2017/09/19/trump-un-speech-2017-full-text-transcript-242879.

Vicedo, Christian Oller. Philippines–U.S. Alliance under the Duterte and Trump Administrations, December 29, 2017. *NDCP Executive Policy Brief.* Retrieved from www.ndcp.edu.ph/wp-content/uploads/publications/EPB_2017-02_Vicedo_Philippine-U.S.%20Security%20Relations.pdf.

Wakefield, Jane. Russia 'Successfully Tests' its Unplugged Internet. September 24, 2019. BBC. Retrieved from https://www.bbc.com/news/technology-50902496

Walt, Stephen M. *The Origins of Alliances.* Ithaca, NY: Cornell University Press, 1987.

Walt, Stephen M. *The Hell of Good Intentions: America's Foreign Policy Elite and the Decline of U.S. Primacy.* New York: Straus and Giroux, 2018.

Waltz, Kenneth N. The Emerging Structure of International Politics. Fall 1993. *International Security*, 18(1): 44–79.

War on the Rocks. Open Letter on Donald Trump from GOP National Security Leaders. March 2, 2016. Retrieved from https://warontherocks.com/2016/03/open-letter-on-donald-trump-from-gop-national-security-leaders/.

White House. The National Security Strategy of the United States of America. September 2002. Retrieved from https://2009-2017.state.gov/documents/organization/63562.pdf.

White House. National Security Strategy of the United States of America. December 2017. Retrieved from https://www.whitehouse.gov/wp-content/uploads/2017/12/NSS-Final-12-18-2017-0905.pdf.

White House. Remarks by President Trump at Signing of the U.S.–China Phase One Trade Agreement. January 15, 2020. Retrieved from https://www.whitehouse.gov/briefings-statements/remarks-president-trump-signing-u-s-china-phase-one-trade-agreement-2/.

Wintour, Patrick. Don't Interfere on Human Rights, says Chinese Envoy before Xi's UK Visit. October 15, 2015. *The Guardian.* Retrieved from https://www.theguardian.com/politics/2015/oct/15/human-rights-chinese-ambassador-xi-jinping-uk-state-visit.

World Economic Forum. A Conversation with Henry Kissinger on the World in 2017. January 21, 2017. Retrieved from https://www.weforum.org/events/world-economic-forum-annual-meeting-2017/sessions/86544.

Zakaria, Fareed. The New China Scare: Why America Shouldn't Panic About Its Latest Challenger. January/February 2020. *Foreign Affairs*. Retrieved from https://www.foreignaffairs.com/articles/china/2019-12-06/new-china-scare.

Zanotti, Jim, and Clayton Thomas. Turkey: Background, U.S. Relations, and Sanctions in Brief. November 8, 2019. Retrieved from https://fas.org/sgp/crs/mideast/R44000.pdf.

5 Agency versus structure and Trumpism's implications for the future

Agency and structure

A key enquiry that motivated this book regarded the manner in which agency and (domestic and international) structure exert influence on the Trump administration's statecraft. Compelling evidence suggests that both interact to produce foreign policy outcomes and, arguably, it is increasingly difficult to discern whether the individual agency of the president or international structure holds greater sway in terms of impact. This suggests that debates considering agency versus structure should not ignore the fact that domestic forces are inherently connected to international structure; in a sense, forces at the domestic and international levels may be 'collapsing' and increasingly interwoven as a result of globalization (with globalization understood here as a fundamental change in the nature or playing field of the international system). This speaks to the case that reacting to issues at either level necessarily has implications for the other. For example, addressing a domestic economic issue relevant to the president's base – such as slowing the loss of US manufacturing jobs – cannot be accomplished without adjusting important international trading relationships. Furthermore, while 'unfair' international trading arrangements were a concern for Trump long before he became president, in the 2016 election Hillary Clinton, and her chief Democrat competitor, Bernie Sanders, also spoke out on the need to reassess certain aspects of America's trading relationships with the world. Notably, both pledged to withdraw the US from the TPP (even though Clinton had previously been a proponent of this agreement during her tenure as Secretary of State (2009 to 2013)). Domestic–international structural concerns were clearly factors all candidates took into account. It may be prudent, therefore, for future research on this topic to not separate domestic forces from international structure in analysis, but rather to resurrect the term 'intermestic' first coined by Bayless Manning in 1977 (Manning, 1977).

A subsidiary question is to what extent is the collapse driven by the Trump administration and to what extent is it being driven by globalization? In his 2015 speech launching his campaign for the White House, Trump focused on issues traditionally deemed international – migration, terrorism, trade, and defense. Given his electoral success, did Trump's supporters understand the link between the domestic and international? Alternatively, did his rhetoric and policy proposals convince them that a link existed, and thus they endorsed his platform by supporting him for president (a development that would be another testament to Trump's agency in this case)? In coming presidential elections will the link between the domestic and international remain, or is this an artifact of the Trump campaign style?

The explanation for Trump's policy vis-à-vis Russia stems from either the individual level or systemic level, given there was no domestic political coalition or group in the US that, at least overtly, was pushing for improved US–Russian ties in 2016. It may very well be related to both and while most commentary and scholarship links it to the individual level, Chapter 4 of this book made the case that it is explicable as a response to multipolarity. Arguably, the same holds for NATO. There was no obvious domestic political constituency in 2016 that sought to change America's approach to NATO even if getting US allies to pay more for their defense equated with the US paying less according to Trump, a position that would have played well within the general economic narrative of grievance Trump crafted and that connected with parts of the electorate. Indeed, public polling showed that while a majority of voters wanted the US to pay more attention to dealing with its own affairs, there was still majority support for US alliances (Brands, 2018, 87). Changes in this area are likely attributable to the president's individual preferences and/or, as argued in Chapter 4, a response to structural pressures – a case supported by the fact that many recent US presidents and officials have complained about allied free-riding.

The general motivation behind the administration's desire to adjust certain agreements or establish new ones to deliver greater benefits to the US are also not out of step with a system-level explanation: A superpower facing an emergent multipolar system and relative decline should be expected to try to derive more power. However, the causal explanation for the method through which Trump has done this – hard-line negotiations and unpredictable behavior – would appear to be Trump's personality. Structure creates pressures; individuals decide how to respond to them based upon their individual preferences and, usually, by considering how it will interact with domestic factors.

What is fascinating here, however, is that two US presidents – Trump and Nixon – acted unpredictably or irrationally during periods of relative US decline and emerging multipolarity. There is not space here to consider whether the psychological profile of both Trump and Nixon is similar enough to confirm that they responded to comparable structural incentives in the same way. More research on this issue would be informative. Henry Kissinger is one direct personal link between the two administrations. In the Nixon administration, he was instrumental in the American strategy of realpolitik and outreach to China to shift the balance of power away from the Soviet Union at a critical time; he appears to have had some influence over president Trump's thinking on foreign policy, and perhaps reinforced the president's morally ambivalent view of the world and his attempt to shift towards a Kissingerian strategy. Here, we would benefit from additional research into the role Kissinger has played in shaping Trump's thinking and in the administration's attitude towards the world, and into whether Kissinger, at the tactical level, actively encouraged Nixon and Trump to adopt unpredictability as a working method to generate leverage and keep other states off-balance.

Evaluating the president's tactics and strategy

The book also set itself the task of assessing the results of the president's tactics and strategy, and whether we learn anything about how effective he is in addressing systemic needs. Regardless of an analyst's opinion of Trump's politics, a dimension of policy consideration will inevitably be missing from any evaluation which is unwilling to discuss policy in the context of the policymakers' goals. In the absence of such appraisal, it will be that much harder to identify the logic of any government and formulate a reasonable idea of what policies it may be likely to pursue in the future. Chapters 2 and 3 outlined the results of such an evaluation. To briefly recount them: as of March 9, 2020, the president can point to a number of moderate successes. He has not achieved the fullest extent of what he promised nor has he fallen as short as some critics like to argue. On trade, NAFTA was replaced by the USMCA, which will make a small contribution to the US economy. The US–China trade war eased marginally after the Phase I deal was signed. In doing so, it addressed some concerns in the trading relationship on the US side, although by all accounts the truly thorny issue of Chinese structural reform is where the major gains lie. In theory, a Phase II agreement would address this but it will require extremely difficult negotiations that will test the mettle and skill of Trump and his negotiators, and the extent to which they are prepared to compromise. Potentially, it will require a broader political breakthrough in relations with Beijing – China may very well only feel comfortable making significant structural economic changes if they are combined with a new international political–security relationship with Washington that recognizes China's expanding global ambitions. Given the increasingly tense competition between the US and China, one where some American officials (not Trump) are promoting ideological differences between Washington and Beijing to the forefront, US–Chinese relations appear primed for the Blob to hem in the president (as it has on Russia) should it judge he is seeking to alter relations with Beijing in a way it finds undesirable to secure a Phase II deal.

On NATO, an increase in spending was already on the cards before Trump's presidency, with central and eastern European states, especially, ramping up spending chiefly in response to the Russian threat. Perhaps Trump's pressure has ensured that most NATO members have not reduced their spending commitments. But even some major economies, such as Italy and France, have not increased their expenditure from 2015 levels. Indeed, bucking US pressure may be viewed as a domestic political boon for their leaders. One clear success (albeit largely symbolic given the relatively small amount it saves the US) was changing the balance of contributions by NATO members towards NATO's central budget. One area of major concern is that America's European NATO allies are overtly expressing a desire to shift to a posture of greater strategic autonomy from the United States. Whether this is considered a negative development to the Trump administration is an open question – a strategy that seeks to reduce the US role in the world, as called for by many realists and those in the 'restraint constituency', requires US allies to fill power vacuums. The US would much prefer European states to carry more of the global security burden than, say, Russia (as long as it is an adversary) and especially China. However, at worst, a more militarily powerful Europe risks a rift in the Western security architecture if European states hard balance against American power. Greater European military power would also imply that any future shift in European intentions vis-à-vis the US would be significant – a Europe hostile to the US without a credible autonomous military capability would be a nuisance; one that translates the combined weight of Europe's economy into a substantial increase in military power with greater nuclear capabilities could be an existential concern. Albeit unlikely, the prospect is no longer unthinkable and that, in itself, is striking.

A geopolitical coup for Washington in the context of the US–China competition would be turning Russia away from Beijing and towards the West. The structural pressure to do so is obvious: An overt military alliance between Russia and China, which is distinctly plausible given the current trajectory of their relations, would immensely expand the power of Moscow and Beijing at the expense of the US and the broader Western alliance. So far, efforts by the Trump administration, and in particular by the president himself, have made no headway in shifting the triangle of relations between the US, Russia, and China. In fact, the trends show China and Russia continuing their slow march towards a military alliance. Here, the influence at the domestic level of the foreign policy bureaucracy has derailed efforts to improve US–Russian ties and, seemingly, set the US on course for a protracted confrontation against a new Chinese–Russian entente. The consequences of this could be severe: Moscow and Beijing, no longer compelled to deploy military forces along their border to deter or defend against one another in a military contingency, are able to free up those forces to place pressure, in Russia's case, on former Soviet states and eastern/central Europe to bend to its desires, and for China to expand its naval power out into the Pacific. Moreover, they both strengthen one another through sustained and growing economic, energy, and technological trade.

Therefore, from an international perspective the administration's record is mixed. There are some moderate successes that could be built upon, alongside failures and areas where relations have come to a standstill (such as in negotiations with North Korea). Domestically, in terms of the president's electoral fortunes, his foreign policy record may have slightly improved them. In early February 2020, the president experienced his highest level of support among Republicans, with 94% approving of his performance (Jones, 2020). This comes in the wake of recent successes that play to his policy of improving the terms of trade for the US, such as the signing of the USMCA and Phase I trade deal with China. However, it also comes against the backdrop of a robust economy and prominent domestic controversies, such as an impeachment trial that could have resulted in an uptick in Trump's popularity. Additionally, from mid-December 2017 through to this writing (March 9, 2020) Trump's aggregate RealClearPolitics approval rating poll has run between 37.1% and 46.3% (the latter figure was reached on February 25, 2020) (RealClearPolitics, 2020). Again, what causally contributed to the recent bump is difficult to discern given multiple conditions and issues. At the margins, it is possible his international performance has played a role.

Trumpism's implications for the future

Modeling hard-line negotiations and unpredictability

Trump's hard-line negotiation strategy and generally unethical behavior could have implications for how states practice international relations. Social learning theory explains that observers can adopt the unethical conduct of "models" if they are not penalized for it, creating norms where the behavior is acceptable (Coleman, 2019, 231). Trump, with his 73.4 million Twitter followers and ability to command the attention of the US and international media, has a modeling megaphone of global reach. Turning to his method of negotiation, his approach reveals a preference for unilateralism – the US makes a forceful move to compel foreign interlocutors to engage in negotiations with the US rather than confiding with them over the desirability for change and then, collectively, the group opting to change arrangements. If other states perceive the US to have benefited from this, it could breed mimicry, with other powers seeking to unilaterally compel weaker states to adjust their relations/rewrite agreements that they view as unfair. It may be enough for some leaders to decide on this course of action if they perceive it will produce domestic political gains. The US, under the Trump administration, may even turn a blind eye to allies doing this or even support it. Indeed, Trump has already showered praise on UK Prime Minister Boris Johnson for being "tough" in the face of what will be difficult negotiations with continental Europe over Brexit (Payne and Bienkov, 2019), and praised Israeli Prime Minister Benjamin Netanyahu for being "tough, smart and strong" (Halbfinger, 2019).

Speaking on how to counteract Trump's pressure, Trump's former attorney George Ross wrote that organizations or, by extension, governments must "stand your ground" (Shell, 2019, 33). This is logical. If enough states throughout the international system were to do this, we could imagine it would lead to the failure of unilateral efforts to compel change. However, this assumes that weaker states are willing to suffer the costs of non-compliance and/or to run the risk the stronger power is bluffing when it says it will withdraw from major agreements. Mexico and Canada were clearly not willing to run this risk (or only willing to run it for so long) in negotiations with the US over NAFTA; it is an open question whether other states will do the same if stronger powers in their regions start using Trump's negotiation tactics. Finally, by being the more powerful actor in relation to every other state in the international system, the US is able to absorb more costs than any other country if negotiations fail or, for example, if its application of leverage, such as tariffs against China, causes damage to the US and Chinese economy. While we can speculate that domestic political considerations could force a rapid shift in the Trump administration's approach over trade wars if, say, a global recession broke out, in the absence of this or powerful bipartisan opposition, Trump has room to continue to apply pressure.

Trump's erratic behavior and unpredictability may produce a positive pay-off for the US. By keeping states off-guard and uncertain how he will react, they may be less willing to engage in aggressive or assertive moves abroad. For example, the successful strike against Soleimani added substance to Trump's unpredictability, and may have rendered future threats to use force more credible, strengthening US deterrence. However, it is also possible that competitions in one-upmanship in the unpredictability stakes will produce a crisis that spirals out of control, as miscalculation leads to conflict when neither side desired it. For example, while a case can be made that North Korea, unable to read Trump to the same degree it could other presidents, has been careful not to escalate tensions despite the breakdown in negotiations, we cannot rule out that they will return to an aggressive posture in the future, engaging their usual recipe of taunts, threats, and erratic behavior. In turn, if recent experience is any guide, the US president will feel compelled to respond to this with his own brand of unpredictability. Whether a new crisis escalates only to de-escalate is anyone's guess – the chance two unpredictable actors will miscalculate the other's intentions would appear to be larger than if one or both are more predictable. We could also imagine the leaders of states in regional contests employing unpredictable tactics if they believe Trump is being successful in his efforts. A system where multiple states perceive acting unpredictably to be a useful tactic would cause immense global instability. These speculations aside, if the basic goal of the president was to create an impression that he is unpredictable, and to make tactical decisions in the belief that others always have to factor this in (encouraging them to be cautious), then he has certainly been successful. As one allied official reportedly said, "Washington, D.C., is now the epicenter of instability in the world" (Brands, 2017, 24).

The survival of the liberal international order

Will the liberal international order survive? By this stage it appears certain that the order, perhaps with some modifications, will survive

Trump's tenure. How liberal it will be is an open question (and some, such as Andrew Bacevich (2018), have questioned whether the liberal moniker, in light of history, has any real validity in terms of defining the post-war global order). After all, the president seems far more interested in altering its existing arrangements rather than destroying the order outright. It is perhaps instructive here to return to Kissinger, who once explained that the US approach during the Nixon administration was to erect "a new building while tearing down the old beams and not letting the structure collapse" (Brands, 2014, 60). Elaborating on Nixon and Kissinger's plan, Brands (2014, 60) explains:

> This would be accomplished not by standing athwart historical change, but by deftly exploiting it to create new sources of strength and maneuver. The United States would draw its chief adversaries into a more manageable triangular relationship, shed unsustainable commitments while maintaining credibility, and ultimately position itself as the pivot of a more stable and advantageous global balance. Through dynamic and purposeful statecraft, America would transcend its moment of relative decline.

Additionally, Nixon and Kissinger charged that "traditional ethics and morality" had to be set aside if the US was to use creative leadership, and the necessary changes required an "extraordinary concentration of power" in the hands of America's foreign policy leaders (Ibid.). This book has catalogued a number of views and initiatives pursued by the Trump administration that are consistent with the above characterization. Furthermore, Pompeo, while criticizing aspects of the international order and multilateralism for becoming "as an end unto itself" (Pompeo, 2018), has said the US is seeking to rally "the noble nations of the world to build a new liberal order that prevents war and achieves greater prosperity for all" (Ibid.). Ultimately, it is an open question whether the Trump administration will be successful in this effort or whether the changes and uncertainty it generates produce centrifugal forces that derail the creation of a new order.

Final reflections

Immediately prior to signing the Phase I trade deal with China, Trump spoke of international affairs as "a very, very beautiful game of chess, or a game of poker … I can't use the word 'checkers' because it's far greater than any checker game that I've ever seen. But it's a very beautiful mosaic" (White House, 2020). He went on to praise both the Chinese and US negotiators for being "very tough" and, in Trumpian fashion, cast no aspersions on China regarding its management of its domestic affairs or for the ideological differences between Washington and Beijing, stating that "China has developed a political system and a model of economic development that suits its national reality" (Ibid.). The president, at times like this, provides a succinct view of how he views the social world and, by extension, the broader fabric of international relations: To Trump it is a world of morally ambiguous agents engaged in a competition for victory – but also one where business and common interests can lead to deals, so long as he judges them to clearly benefit his own, and America's, material interests.

Indeed, in essence, the statement above also touches upon the fact there are multiple pressures and drivers, gambles and wagers that are taken into account by statesmen and stateswomen. In turn, all of these influence how governments collaborate and compete with one another throughout the international system. As such, this book has tried to decipher key aspects of the president's foreign policy by using multiple levels of analysis. It finds that the structural forces – domestic and international – create constraints and pressures that influence the president's objectives. Likewise, he is reacting to structural forces and seeking to bend international outcomes in his preferred direction. All of this has been on display since Trump's presidency began in 2017.

History will judge how good Trump is at playing the "beautiful game" of international relations, and whether the strengths and weaknesses embodied by the methods and rhetoric he uses to achieve his ends ultimately empower the US or leave it worse off. Indeed, to Trump, how it affects the rest of the world is not the primary concern of an 'America First' foreign policy. Accordingly, this compels the analyst to adjust their frame of reference to consider whether the president has been successful in terms of his and his administration's objectives. In considering this, the book has found Trump and his administration to be moderately successful in achieving their aims but have fallen short of the full extent of outcomes they no doubt hoped for. Will another year or five of a Trump administration make additional headway, and will its successes turn out, after all, to deliver larger and more significant benefits? Achieving substantial gains will require the president to find a better way to work with the foreign policy bureaucracy – his instinct and tenacity will only go so far in the face of its opposition. At worst, it will prevent the US from appropriately adjusting to the powerful forces of multipolarity, and the need to manage a new era of great power competition. In this, the US needs to ensure America's allies remain onside while at the same time multipolarity suggests greater flexibility is necessary to expand the prospects of working cooperatively with new partners; contradictions for statecraft abound.

The world and America's place in it stand at a pivotal inflection point – whether this president and his administration, or future ones, are canny enough to successfully navigate a period of international and domestic political upheaval is an open question. Having once said "My whole life is a bet" (Bennett, 2019), President Trump is gambling that the risks inherent in his unorthodox approach and willingness to challenge traditional foreign policy precepts will produce far more net gains than losses. Only time will tell.

Bibliography

Bacevich, Andrew J. The 'Global Order' Myth. In (eds.) Jervis, Robert, et al. *Chaos in the Liberal Order: The Trump Presidency and International Politics in the Twenty-First Century.* New York: Columbia University Press, 2018.

Bennett, Brian. 'My Whole Life Is a Bet'. Inside President Trump's Gamble on an Untested Re-Election Strategy. June 20, 2019. *Time.* Retrieved from https://time.com/magazine/us/5610714/july-1st-2019-vol-194-no-1-u-s/.

Brands, Hal. *What Good Is Grand Strategy? Power and Purpose in American Statecraft from Harry S. Truman to George W. Bush.* New York: Cornell University Press, 2014.

Brands, Hal. The Unexceptional Superpower: American Grand Strategy in the Age of Trump. 2017. *Survival,* 59(6): 7–40.

Brands, Hal. *American Grand Strategy in the Age of Trump.* Washington, DC: Brookings Institution Press, 2018.

Coleman, Peter T. Tentative Teachings on Conflict from Trump's Tumultuous Tenure in Office. January 2019. *Negotiation Journal,* 35(1): 231–234.

Halbfinger, David M. Netanyahu–Trump Partnership Is Stronger Than Ever. Are These Its Final Days? February 28, 2019. *New York Times.* Retrieved from https://www.nytimes.com/2019/03/10/world/middleeast/netanyahu-trump-election-scandal.html.

Jones, Jeffrey M. Trump Job Approval at Personal Best 49%. February 4, 2020. *Gallup.* Retrieved from https://news.gallup.com/poll/284156/trump-job-approval-personal-best.aspx.

Manning, Bayless. The Congress, the Executive and Intermestic Affairs: Three Proposals. 1977. *Foreign Affairs,* 55(2): 306–324.

Payne, Adam, and Adam Bienkov. Donald Trump Welcomes Boris Johnson's Victory as the 'Britain Trump'. July 24, 2019. *Business Insider.* Retrieved from https://www.businessinsider.com.au/donald-trump-says-boris-johnson-is-smart-tough-and-britain-trump-2019-7?r=US&IR=T.

Pompeo, Mike. Remarks by Secretary Pompeo at the German Marshall Fund. December 4, 2018. https://ua.usembassy.gov/remarks-by-secretary-pompeo-at-the-german-marshall-fund/.

RealClearPolitics. President Trump Job Approval. February 20, 2020. Retrieved from https://www.realclearpolitics.com/epolls/other/president_trump_job_approval-6179.html.

Shell, G. Richard. Transactional Man: Teaching Negotiation Strategy in the Age of Trump. 2019. *Negotiation Journal*, 35(1): 31–45.

White House. Remarks by President Trump at Signing of the U.S.–China Phase One Trade Agreement. January 15, 2020. Retrieved From https://www.whitehouse.gov/briefings-statements/remarks-president-trump-signing-u-s-china-phase-one-trade-agreement-2/.

Index

Page numbers followed by 'n' refer to notes.

For Product Safety Concerns and Information please contact our EU
representative GPSR@taylorandfrancis.com
Taylor & Francis Verlag GmbH, Kaufingerstraße 24, 80331 München, Germany